# バラク・オバマの
## BARACK OBAMA
### スピリチュアル・メッセージ

**再選大統領は世界に平和をもたらすか**

# Spiritual Message from Barack Obama
### Can the Re-elected president really bring world peace?

大川隆法
RYUHO OKAWA

# バラク・オバマの
# スピリチュアル・メッセージ

再選大統領は世界に平和をもたらすか

Spiritual Message from Barack Obama
—— Can the Re-elected president really bring world peace? ——

*Preface*

Who, really, can understand these contents?

If I, the author of this book, were an American, I would get a lightning-like shock from this *Spiritual Interview with Re-elected President Obama*, I agree.

This interview was held this November 8 in Japan, which means November 7 in U.S.A. The place of interview was at the General Headquarters of Happy Science in Tokyo, Japan. The audience, and at the same time witnesses, were about 100. Japanese people heard the Spiritual Message from Re-elected President Barack Obama directly in English. Unbelievable! But, it is the Truth.

I am the Master of the World. So, Miracle is a daily work for me. Anyway, please read the following message.

November 13, 2012
Master & CEO of Happy Science
Ryuho Okawa

## まえがき

　いったい誰がこの内容を理解できるだろうか。

　もし、本書の著者である私自身がアメリカ人であったならば、この『バラク・オバマのスピリチュアル・メッセージ──再選大統領は世界に平和をもたらすか──』に、稲妻に打たれたような衝撃を受けることだろう。同感である。

　このインタビューは、日本時間の11月8日、アメリカ時間の11月7日に収録された。そして、インタビューを収録した場所は、東京の幸福の科学総合本部であり、その聴衆、目撃者は100名にのぼる。日本人は、再選した大統領バラク・オバマ（守護霊）の霊言を直接英語で聴いた。信じ難いことだ！　しかし、それが真実なのだ。

　私は、世界の教師である。だから、私にとって奇跡は、"日々の仕事"である。とまれ、このメッセージを読んでいただきたい。

2012年11月13日

人類の教師・幸福の科学総裁
大川隆法

# Contents

Preface 2

## Chapter One: Spiritual Interview with Re-elected President Obama

1 Asking Obama's Guardian Spirit about His Vision
   of a "Strong America" 16

2 Obama's Wish: Cut the Military Budget
   and Save the Poor 42

3 Politics is an Art of Words 54

4 A Vision of America Becoming a Superpower Again 72

5 Obama Aims to Create a "Japanese-Type Socialism"
   That Has a Big Middle-Class 88

6 Which One First: Educating the Poor or Creating
   a New Industry? 100

目　次

まえがき　　3

## 第1章　再選したオバマ大統領の
　　　　　スピリチュアル・インタビュー

1　オバマ守護霊に、「強いアメリカ」
　　のビジョンを訊く　　17

2　「軍事予算を削減し、
　　貧しい人々を助けたい」という願い　　43

3　政治とは「言葉の技術」である　　55

4　アメリカを再び
　　超大国にするための構想　　73

5　目指しているのは、
　　中流階級の多い"日本型の社会主義"　　89

6　「貧困層の教育」が先か、「新産業の創造」が先か　　101

7  President Obama: The Secrets and Tendencies
   of His Soul                                              112

8  Xi Jinping is Like the Reincarnation of Mao Zedong  128

9  President Obama is Planning to Prioritize Education
   and Increase Taxes on the Wealthy                   134

10 President Obama Will Need to Consider GOP's
   Opinions Under the "Divided Congress"               142

11 A Secretary of State Other than Hillary May
   Accelerate Chinese Expansionism                     146

12 Japan Must Strengthen Their Self-Defense            156


# Chapter Two: Discourse with Obama

―― An Interview with the Guardian Spirit of Obama ――

1  Summoning Mr. Obama's Guardian Spirit              166
2  He Has No Idea on How to Solve America's Financial
   Problems                                            174
3  My Main Concern is America's Domestic Issues       178

7　オバマ大統領の魂の秘密と傾向性　　113

8　習近平氏は
　　「毛沢東が生まれ変わったような人物」　　129

9　教育を重視し、富裕層への増税を
　　考えているオバマ大統領　　135

10　「ねじれ議会」の下では、ある程度、
　　共和党に配慮せざるをえない　　143

11　ヒラリー氏以外の国務長官では、
　　中国の増長を許す可能性がある　　147

12　日本は自主防衛を強化したほうがよい　　157

## 第2章　オバマとの対話
―――オバマ守護霊インタビュー―――

1　オバマ氏の守護霊を招霊する　　167
2　金融危機を救うアイデアはない　　175

3　主な関心は「アメリカ国内」にある　　179

| | |
|---|---|
| 4 I Want to Speak with the Great China Rather than Japan | 180 |
| 5 I am Not Interested in Korea and Taiwan | 184 |
| 6 America Will No Longer be The World Policeman | 186 |
| 7 Are Rich People Evil Existences? | 192 |
| 8 His True Feelings: The Japanese are Sneaky People | 194 |
| 9 Is China the Future of America? | 200 |
| 10 He Wants to Become a President More Famous than Lincoln | 208 |
| 11 You Must Govern Your Nation by Yourself | 214 |
| 12 It's Time for Revenge | 216 |
| Afterword | 220 |

4　日本よりも「偉大な中国」と話がしたい　　181

5　朝鮮と台湾については関心がない　　185
6　将来、アメリカは「世界の警察」
　　ではなくなる　　187
7　富裕層は「邪悪な存在」？　　193
8　「日本はアメリカの敵」という本音　　195
9　「中国はアメリカの未来」なのか　　201
10　リンカン以上の有名な大統領になりたい　　209

11　自分たちの力で自国を治めるのが原則だ　　215
12　今こそ、リベンジのとき　　217

## あとがき　　221

This book is the transcript of spiritual messages given by the guardian spirits of American President Barack Obama.

These spiritual messages were channeled through Ryuho Okawa. However, please note that because of his high level of enlightenment, his way of receiving spiritual messages is fundamentally different from other psychic mediums who undergo trances and are completely taken over by the spirits they are channeling.

Each human soul is made up of six soul siblings, one of whom acts as the guardian spirit of the person living on earth. People living on earth are connected to their guardian spirits at the innermost subconscious level. They are a part of people's very souls, and therefore, are an exact reflection of their thoughts and philosophies.

Please note that these spiritual messages are opinions of the individual spirits and may contradict the ideas or teachings of the Happy Science Group.

These spiritual messages were given in English, but Chapter 1, Sections 9 to 12 were spoken in Japanese. English translations are provided for these parts.

本書は、アメリカ合衆国大統領バラク・オバマ氏の守護霊の霊言を収録したものである。
　「霊言現象」とは、あの世の霊存在の言葉を語り下ろす現象のことをいう。これは高度な悟りを開いた者に特有のものであり、「霊媒現象」（トランス状態になって意識を失い、霊が一方的にしゃべる現象）とは異なる。

　また、人間の魂は六人のグループからなり、あの世に残っている「魂の兄弟」の一人が守護霊を務めている。つまり、守護霊は、実は自分自身の魂の一部である。
　したがって、「守護霊の霊言」とは、いわば、本人の潜在意識にアクセスしたものであり、その内容は、その人が潜在意識で考えていること（本心）と考えてよい。
　ただ、「霊言」は、あくまでも霊人の意見であり、幸福の科学グループとしての見解と矛盾する内容を含む場合がある点、付記しておきたい。
　なお、今回、霊人の発言は英語にて行われた。本書は、それに日本語訳を付けたものである（ただし、第1章9〜12節は日本語にて行われ、それに英訳を付けている）。

# Chapter One:
# Spiritual Interview with Re-elected President Obama

November 8, 2012, at Happy Science General Headquarters
Spiritual Messages from the Guardian Spirit of Barack Obama

# 第1章
# 再選したオバマ大統領の
# スピリチュアル・インタビュー

2012年11月8日 幸福の科学総合本部にて
バラク・オバマ守護霊の霊示

Barack Hussein Obama, Jr. (1961 ～ )

The 44th President of the United States. Born in Hawaii, he is an American politician and a member of the Democratic Party. After graduating Harvard Law School, he worked as a civil rights attorney in Chicago. In 2004, he won the general election for the US Senate and in 2008 was elected as the first African-American president of the United States. In 2012 he won his second term in office following the closely contested presidential elections against the Republican candidate, Mitt Romney.

**Interviewer**

Kazuhiro Ichikawa
   Senior Managing Director
   Chief Director of International Headquarters

Shugaku Tsuiki
   Happiness Realization Party Leader

Toshihisa Sakakibara
   Managing Director
   Director General of El Cantare Belief Promotion Division

※Position titles are at the time of interview.

バラク・フセイン・オバマ Jr.（1961 ～）
アメリカ合衆国の政治家。民主党に所属。第44代大統領。ハワイ州出身。ハーバード大学ロースクールを修了後、シカゴで人権派弁護士として活動する。2004年、上院議員に当選。2008年の大統領選挙で、アメリカ初の黒人大統領となる。二期目を目指した2012年の大統領選挙では、接戦の末、共和党のミット・ロムニー候補に勝利した。

**質問者**
市川和博（幸福の科学専務理事 兼 国際本部長）

立木秀学（幸福実現党党首）

榊原俊尚（幸福の科学常務理事 兼
　　　　　エル・カンターレ信仰伝道局長）

※役職は収録当時のもの

# 1 Asking Obama's Guardian Spirit about His Vision of a "Strong America"

Obama's Guardian Spirit[*]   Hello, Japan!

Audience   Hello.

Obama's G.S.   Hello, my citizens! Welcome to the White House! (*audience laughs*)

MC   Thank you.

Obama's G.S.   Thank you very much.

MC   Now, Master Ryuho Okawa will give us a spiritual interview, "Spiritual Interview with Re-elected President Obama."

Obama's G.S.   Too late. (*audience laughs*)

---

[*] Obama's Guardian Spirit will hereafter be abbreviated as Obama's G.S.

第1章　再選したオバマ大統領のスピリチュアル・インタビュー

# 1　オバマ守護霊に、「強いアメリカ」のビジョンを訊く

オバマ守護霊　日本のみなさん、こんにちは！

会場　こんにちは。

オバマ守護霊　国民のみなさん、こんにちは。"ホワイトハウス"へ、ようこそ（会場笑）。

司会　ありがとうございます。

オバマ守護霊　本当にありがとう。

司会　それでは、大川隆法総裁より、「再選したオバマ大統領のスピリチュアル・インタビュー」を賜ります。


オバマ守護霊　遅すぎますよ（会場笑）。

## 1 Spiritual Interview with Re-elected President Obama

**MC**   Yes, it seems to be so.

**Obama's G.S.**   This is my second time, or maybe the third? (The first spiritual interview with President Obama's guardian spirit was recorded on November 5, 2008. See Chapter 2.)

**Ichikawa**   Thank you for inviting us to the White House. We really appreciate you coming here and having an interview with us.

**Obama's G.S.**   Thank you.

**Ichikawa**   Also, congratulations.

**Obama's G.S.**   You are the front-runner and the first interviewer from Japan, right? You're smart.

Are you from a Japanese TV station? NHK? Happy Science TV? No problem.

第1章　再選したオバマ大統領のスピリチュアル・インタビュー

司会　そうですね。

オバマ守護霊　（インタビューは）2回目でしょうか。それとも3回目？（2008年11月5日、オバマ氏の守護霊を招霊し、インタビューを行った。本書第2章に所収）

市川　"ホワイトハウス"にお招きいただき、ありがとうございます。このようなかたちで、私たちとのインタビューの機会を頂きましたことに、たいへん感謝いたします。

オバマ守護霊　ありがとう。

市川　そして、おめでとうございます。

オバマ守護霊　あなたが、第一走者、日本からの最初のインタビュアーですね。あなたは優秀ですね。
　これは、日本のテレビ局ですか。NHK？　ハッピー・サイエンスTVですか。問題ありません。

## 1 Spiritual Interview with Re-elected President Obama

**Ichikawa**  Could you first tell us how you are feeling now?

　First, congratulations on your re-election as the President of the United States of America.

**Obama's G.S.**  Thank you. Thank you for your backup. Thank you. (*audience applauses*)

**Ichikawa**  So, first, could you tell us your feelings now as the President?

**Obama's G.S.**  Very happy! I'm happy! It was my goal to win my second term as President. This is definitely my job. I need eight years to complete my job, to make a "Strong America," you know? Of course!

**Ichikawa**  Could you tell us about your vision for a "Strong America"?

第1章　再選したオバマ大統領のスピリチュアル・インタビュー

市川　最初に、今のお気持ちをお聞かせいただけますか。

　まず初めに、アメリカ大統領への再選、おめでとうございます。

オバマ守護霊　ありがとう。みなさんのご支援に感謝します。ありがとう（会場拍手）。

市川　それでは、最初に、大統領としての今のお気持ちをお聞かせいただけますか。

オバマ守護霊　幸せです！　私はハッピーです！　２期目の勝利は、私の目標でした。これは間違いなく私の仕事です。私の仕事を完成させるために、８年は必要なのです。私は、「強いアメリカ」をつくります。知っているでしょう？　当然のことです！

市川　「強いアメリカ」をつくるためのビジョンを教えていただけますか。

## 1 Spiritual Interview with Re-elected President Obama

**Obama's G.S.**   Is this for Happy Science TV? Oh, this is a scoop. Is this CNN or BBC? First of all, who are you? (*audience laughs*)

**Ichikawa**   We are from Happy Science, a religious organization established in 1986 by Master Ryuho Okawa. We are a very big movement that goes beyond the boundaries of religion. Master Okawa gives us directions related to politics, economics, and education.

**Obama's G.S.**   Oh, you speak a lot, and fluently, too. Good! Just like an American! Come to America and become an American citizen, and vote for me! (*audience laughs*)

**Ichikawa**   Thank you. May I introduce the other two interviewers?

**Obama's G.S.**   Oh, he (looking at Tsuiki) might be an enemy. No? (*audience laughs*)

オバマ守護霊　それを、ハッピー・サイエンスTVで言うのですか。これはスクープですよ。CNNやBBCかもしれませんね。そもそも、あなたがたは誰なのですか（会場笑）。

市川　私たちは幸福の科学と申します。1986年に大川隆法総裁が設立された宗教団体であり、宗教の枠を超えた非常に大きな活動を行っております。大川総裁は、政治や経済、教育に関しても方向性を示されています。

オバマ守護霊　たくさん話せるのですね。流暢で、よろしい！　アメリカ人のようですよ。アメリカへ来て、アメリカ国民になり、私に投票しなさい！（会場笑）

市川　ありがとうございます。他の2名のインタビュアーをご紹介してよろしいでしょうか。

オバマ守護霊　（立木に）おお、君は敵かもしれませんね。違いますか（会場笑）。

**Tsuiki**   No, no. My name is Shugaku Tsuiki. The party leader of the Happiness Realization Party.

**Obama's G.S.**   Party killer? (*audience laughs*)

**Tsuiki**   Party *leader*. Leader.

**Obama's G.S.**   Oh, party leader. Yeah, OK.

**Tsuiki**   I am the party leader of the Happiness Realization Party, a Japanese political party. So, Japan and United States have an alliance, so we have very…

**Obama's G.S.**   Speak fluently, please. (*audience laughs*)

**Tsuiki**   We have a great deal of interest in you.

第1章　再選したオバマ大統領のスピリチュアル・インタビュー

立木　いえいえ、違います。私は立木秀学と申します。幸福実現党のパーティー・リーダー（党首）です。

オバマ守護霊　パーティー・キラー（党を殺す人）ですか（会場笑）。

立木　党首、リーダーです。

オバマ守護霊　ああ、党首ですか。分かりました。オーケー。

立木　日本の政党である幸福実現党の党首です。日本とアメリカ合衆国の同盟は、非常に……。

オバマ守護霊　流暢に話してください（会場笑）。

立木　私たちは、あなたに対して、大きな関心を抱いています。

**Obama's G.S.**   Do you stand with me or against me?

**Tsuiki**   No, no. We have an alliance.

**Obama's G.S.**   Alliance? Alliance? OK.

**Tsuiki**   So, I want to ask you a question. I think that the American President has a role to realize justice in the world.

**Obama's G.S.**   American President? A roll?
 Your Japanese-English is difficult. Give me the conclusion.

**Tsuiki**   How will you fulfill your responsibility to realize justice in this world?

**Obama's G.S.**   We have citizens of Japanese origin,

**オバマ守護霊** あなたは、私の味方ですか、それとも敵ですか。

**立木** いいえ、同盟関係にあります。

**オバマ守護霊** 同盟？ 同盟ですか。分かりました。

**立木** 私がお訊きしたいことは、アメリカ大統領には役割があって、「世界の正義を実現する」という役割を持っていると思います。

**オバマ守護霊** アメリカ大統領はロール？
　分かりにくい"日本語英語"ですね。結論は？

**立木** あなたは、世界に対する正義の責務を、どのように果たしていかれますか。

**オバマ守護霊** わが国には、日系の国民もいるので、あ

so I must be kind to you. But your question is a little difficult for me. It sounds like some kind of a riddle. Tell me in a word. What do you want to ask me?

Tsuiki   For example, I would like to ask about China.

Obama's G.S.   China? China is a great country.

Tsuiki   China is an emerging power.

Obama's G.S.   Oh, OK. Be friends with China. That's all. (*audience laughs*)

Tsuiki   But, they have the intention to invade Japan and its surrounding countries.

Obama's G.S.   No, no. They didn't say so.

Tsuiki   To be sure, they didn't say so exactly, but they

なたがたには親切にしなければなりません。しかし、あなたの質問は少し難しくて、謎かけか何かのようです。要するに、何が訊きたいのですか。

立木　例えば、中国に関してです。

オバマ守護霊　中国についてですか。中国は偉大な国です。

立木　中国は新興列強です。

オバマ守護霊　ああ、そうです。中国と友達になりなさい。以上です（会場笑）。

立木　しかし、彼らは日本や周辺国を侵略するつもりです。

オバマ守護霊　いやいや、違います。彼らは、そうは言っていませんよ。

立木　確かに、そうは言っていませんが、彼らは侵略す

have the will to invade…

**Obama's G.S.**  How are you able to say that?

**Tsuiki**  Because they have a…

**Obama's G.S.**  Because the American President is weak?

**Tsuiki**  No, no. They have continued to increase their military budget for decades and their action is very dangerous. For example, the Senkaku islands are our territory, but…

**Obama's G.S.**  Really?

**Tsuiki**  Yes. China admitted that before resources were found under the sea. But after they found out about that, they…

る意志を持っていて……。

**オバマ守護霊** なぜ、そう言えるのですか。

**立木** なぜかというと、彼らは……。

**オバマ守護霊** アメリカ大統領が弱いからですか。

**立木** いえいえ。彼らは、軍事費を何十年も拡大し続けており、彼らの行動は非常に危険です。例えば、尖閣諸島は日本の領土なのですが……。

**オバマ守護霊** 本当に？

**立木** はい。中国はかつて、日本の領土だと認めていました。しかし、海底に資源が発見されると、彼らは……。

1 Spiritual Interview with Re-elected President Obama

Obama's G.S.   Please say those things to China.

Tsuiki   Yes, we are saying so. And…

Obama's G.S.   Please protest.

Tsuiki   Yes. But they have the intention to invade the surrounding countries. So, this movement is very, very dangerous.

Obama's G.S.   That might be so. But in this context, you shouldn't use the word *dangerous*. In a diplomatic context, the word *dangerous* is dangerous. (*laughs*) You know? *Dangerous* means you are looking down on them as a hidden enemy or something like that. So, please use a more decent word.

Tsuiki   But my English is poor. (*audience laughs*)

Obama's G.S.   No, no. You are clever and fluent

第1章　再選したオバマ大統領のスピリチュアル・インタビュー

オバマ守護霊　それは中国に言ってください。

立木　はい、もちろん言っています。そして……。

オバマ守護霊　中国に訴(うった)えてください。

立木　はい。しかし、彼らは、周辺国を侵略するつもりです。ですから、この動きは非常に危険です。


オバマ守護霊　そうかもしれません。しかし、これに関して、あなたは「危険」という言葉を使ってはいけません。外交においては、「危険」という言葉は、危険です（笑）。分かります？　「危険」というのは、あなたが、彼らを隠(かく)れた敵か、それに近いものとして見下していることを意味します。ですから、もっと礼儀(れいぎ)正しい言葉を使ってください。

立木　しかし、私の英語は拙(つたな)いですので（会場笑）。

オバマ守護霊　いえいえ。あなたは頭がよいですから、

33

in English. You can speak. Of course, you can. If you are going to criticize another country, first, you must admit the fact and then next, please praise them, and after that, criticize one part of them. It's one of the techniques of politics. You started from the conclusion. You want to say, "Attack China!" "Beat down China!" "Kill all Chinese people!"

Tsuiki   No, no, no.

Obama's G.S.   Like that.

Tsuiki   But this is a spiritual interview. So…

Obama's G.S.   Oh, yeah, yeah, spiritual.

Tsuiki   …so you may say what you are thinking.

Obama's G.S.   I understand. You want to say, "All

きっと流暢な英語を話せますよ。もし、あなたが他の国を批判するならば、最初に、事実を認め、次に相手をほめて、その後、一部分を批判しなければなりません。それが政治の技術の一つです。あなたは、最初に、いきなり結論から始めたのです。あなたは、「中国を攻撃せよ！ 中国を屈服させよ！ 中国人を全員殺せ！」というようなことを言いたいのでしょう。

立木　違います。

オバマ守護霊　そんな感じでしょう。

立木　しかし、これは霊的なインタビューですので……。

オバマ守護霊　ああ、分かりました。霊的なものですね。

立木　ですから、あなたも自分の考えをおっしゃっていただいて構いません。

オバマ守護霊　分かりましたよ。あなたは、「中国人全員

Chinese should be spiritual beings." That's your intention. "They should not live in this earthly world. They should go to the spiritual world." (*audience laughs*) Oh! You are a religion. Splendid! (*laughs*)

**Tsuiki**  No, no. We hope to have a friendly relationship with China.

**Obama's G.S.**  Really? Relationship with them?

**Tsuiki**  But they intend to attack Japan.

**Obama's G.S.**  No, no. Please go to China and say, "Hello Chinese people. Be friends with me. Be friends with our party." Please say that first, and after that, if you want to say something more, please add to that. First, you want to be friends with your enemy. It is a teaching of Jesus Christ and of Ryuho Okawa, so, please follow those teachings.

が霊的存在になるべきだ」と言いたいのでしょう。それが本音ですね。「彼らは地上世界に住むべきではなく、霊界に還るべきだ」ということですね(会場笑)。オー、"宗教"だ。素晴らしい！(笑)

立木　いいえ、そうではありません。私たちは、中国と友好関係を持ちたいと願っています。

オバマ守護霊　本当ですか。彼らと友好関係を？

立木　しかし、彼らは、日本を攻撃する意図を持っています。

オバマ守護霊　いや、違います。中国に行って、「中国のみなさん、こんにちは。私と友達になってください。私たちの政党と仲良くしてください」と言えばよいのです。最初にそう言って、そのあとに、もし何か言いたいことがあるならば、付け加えるんですよ。まず、敵と友達になろうとすることです。これは、イエス・キリストの教えですし、大川隆法さんの教えでもあります。教えを守ってください。

**Tsuiki**  I don't agree with you. At the very least, Master Ryuho Okawa never gave such teachings.

**Obama's G.S.**  Master Okawa is a great person, I know because I was interviewed already.

But he predicted that my presidency would cause the decline of the United States of America and that prediction is 100% *correct* (*The Sun Will Always Rise*, January 2009, by IRH Press co., Ltd. Only available in Japanese). Not so good (*whacks table with book*) . Too much accuracy is akin to bad emotion or bad desire. So, predictions should be 50/50.

Do you understand what I'm saying? So, if a splendid religious person predicts the future, there must be some condition regarding the realization of that prediction.

Do you understand my use of the term *condition*? Without conditions, the prediction is a fate ordered by God. There are no efforts required from us human

## 第1章　再選したオバマ大統領のスピリチュアル・インタビュー

立木　それには賛成できません。少なくとも、大川隆法総裁は、そんなことはおっしゃっていません。

**オバマ守護霊**　大川先生は、偉大な人です。すでにインタビューされたことがあるから知っています。

　しかし、彼は、私の大統領任期中にアメリカ合衆国が衰退(すいたい)することを予言し、その予言は100パーセント的中しました（2009年1月発刊『朝の来ない夜はない』〔幸福の科学出版刊〕等参照）。これはいいことではありません（本でテーブルを叩(たた)く）。予言があまりに正確なのは、悪い感情や悪い願望のようなものです。ですから、予言は五分五分であるべきです。

　私の言っていることが分かりますか。もし、素晴らしい宗教家が未来を予言する場合には、予言の実現に関して、何らかの条件を付けるべきなのです。

　私の使っている「条件」という言葉の意味が理解できますか。条件がないのなら、その予言は、神の下された運命になってしまいます。つまり、そこには、われわれ

1 Spiritual Interview with Re-elected President Obama

beings. So it is like an order from God or a fate that God decided. This kind of prediction is not so welcomed.

So, if you use such kind of prediction, please add some condition to that. For example, you could say, "If Barack Obama does well as a President of the United States, he will succeed, but if he fails, the economy of the United States will go down," or something like that. It is a common rule of predictions, you know?

**Tsuiki** But Master Okawa analyzed the tendency of your soul.

**Obama's G.S.** Analyzed?

**Tsuiki** Yes, and based on this analysis, he predicted the decline of America. So…

**Obama's G.S.** No, no, it's not my fault. I did my best

人間に、何の努力も求められていないのです。そのような、神からの命令、神が定められた運命という類の予言は、あまり歓迎されないのです。

　ですから、もし、そうした予言を使うのであれば、何か条件を付けてほしいのです。例えば、「バラク・オバマがアメリカ合衆国大統領として、よい仕事をした場合には、彼は成功するだろう。しかし、もし、彼が失敗したら、アメリカ経済は下降するだろう」といった言い方です。それが予言の共通のルールなのです。分かりますか。


立木　しかし、大川総裁は、あなたの「魂の傾向性」を分析されました。


オバマ守護霊　分析した？


立木　はい。魂の傾向性を分析し、その分析に基づいて、アメリカの衰退を予言されました。ですから……。


オバマ守護霊　いや、違います。それは私のせいではあ

and…

Tsuiki  It's your responsibility. Your responsibility.

Obama's G.S.  I will do my best. My citizens, don't listen to his words. I will do my best. The next four years will be the golden age of the United States of America. That's the reason I won!

Tsuiki  Yes. So, I hope that America will become stronger. I hope to cooperate with you.

# 2 Obama's Wish: Cut the Military Budget and Save the Poor

Tsuiki  May I ask another question? I want to speak to you about the fiscal problem.

Obama's G.S.  The fiscal cliff?
<sub>Note p.54</sub>

りません。私はベストを尽くしました。そして……。

立木　これは、あなたの責任です。あなたの責任なのです。

オバマ守護霊　私はベストを尽くします。わが国民よ、彼の言葉を聞いてはなりません。私はベストを尽くします。次の4年間は、アメリカ合衆国の黄金時代になるでしょう。それが、私が勝利した理由です！

立木　そうですね。私は「強いアメリカ」を望みます。私は、あなたと協力していけることを願っているのです。

## 2 「軍事予算を削減し、貧しい人々を助けたい」という願い

立木　それでは、ここで質問を変えます。財政問題に関して、お訊きしたいと思います。

オバマ守護霊　「財政の崖」のことですか。
注 p.55

1 Spiritual Interview with Re-elected President Obama

**Tsuiki**  Yes, the fiscal cliff. How will you cope with the fiscal cliff?

**Obama's G.S.**  That is next January.

**Tsuiki**  But it needs to be settled by this year.

**Obama's G.S.**  It's one of my weak points, which was attacked by Mitt Romney. But I argued with him and I conquered his criticism, so American people rely on me.

I have skill. I have wisdom. I will have guidance from Heaven. So I will change the fate of the United States and my great desire for prosperity should create the way to the glorious conclusion of the United States.

Please rely on me. Just rely on me. It's enough.

**Tsuiki**  I think the tax cut for rich people should be kept, but you don't want to maintain the tax cut for

立木　ええ、「財政の崖」についてです。あなたは、これに対してどう立ち向かっていかれますか。

オバマ守護霊　それは来年の1月の話ですね。

立木　しかし、この問題は、今年中に解決する必要があります。

オバマ守護霊　それは、ミット・ロムニーに攻撃された弱点の一つです。しかし、私は彼と論争し、彼の批判に勝ったのです。だから、アメリカ国民は、私を信頼しています。
　私にはスキルがあります。知恵があります。天国からの指導もあるでしょう。私は、アメリカ合衆国の運命を変えるつもりです。私の、繁栄への強い願いは、「輝けるアメリカ合衆国」という果実となって現れるでしょう。
　どうか、私を信頼してください。ただ信じてほしいのです。それで十分です。

立木　そのためには、富裕層への減税が維持される必要があると思います。しかし、あなたは富裕層に対する減税を

rich people. This is what caused the decline of the U.S. economy.

**Obama′s G.S.**   No, no. That is just one opinion.

**Tsuiki**   But rich people have…

**Obama′s G.S.**   Wealthy people are affluent. If they are forced to take responsibility for saving the weaker people, they are capable of doing that by paying more than 50% taxes or through other obligations. They can be in charge of that kind of task and it's their mission. It's the mission of wealthy people.

You are a religion and a religious political party; so you should say that this is the mission of wealthy people. They should save the weak and disabled, minorities, and other kinds of unfortunate people. It's a religious order, a religious mission.

You can understand that it's a mission from God,

維持したくないのです。これがアメリカ経済衰退の原因になるでしょう。

**オバマ守護霊** いや、違います。それは一つの見方にすぎません。

**立木** しかし、裕福な人々は……。

**オバマ守護霊** 富裕層は裕福です。もし、彼らが弱者を救済するように強いられたら、50パーセント以上の税金を払うことも、あるいは、他の義務であってもできるでしょう。彼らは、そういう仕事を担うことができるのです。それが、富める者、裕福な人々の使命です。

　あなたがたは、宗教であり、宗教政党なのだから、「それが豊かな人々の使命だ」と言うべきです。彼らが、弱者や障害者、マイノリティー（少数派）などの不幸な人々を救うべきなのです。それが、宗教団体であり、宗教的使命です。
　それが、神から与えられた使命であることぐらい、あ

right? Ryuho Okawa is a friend of Jesus Christ, so he must shake hands with Jesus Christ regarding this matter. You are being deceived by your Master.

Tsuiki   But helping poor people is…

Obama's G.S.   It's essential. It's urgent. It's a severe winter.

Tsuiki   Yes.

Obama's G.S.   There was also a hurricane. And there is another hurricane coming.

Tsuiki   But we do not need to involve the government. Rich people should help poor people without involving the government.

Obama's G.S.   Without the government?

なたにも分かるでしょう。大川隆法さんは、イエス・キリストの友人なのだから、この問題について、イエス・キリストと握手(あくしゅ)しなければならないはずです。あなたは総裁に騙(だま)されているのです。

立木　しかし、貧しい人々を助けることは……。

オバマ守護霊　それが最も大事なことです。差し迫(せま)った問題です。厳しい冬なのです。

立木　はい。

オバマ守護霊　そして、ハリケーンも来ました。次のハリケーンも控(ひか)えているのです。

立木　しかし、そのために政府を巻き込(こ)む必要はありません。富裕層が、政府とは関係なく、貧しい人を助ければよいのです。

オバマ守護霊　政府抜(ぬ)きで？

**Tsuiki**  Yes, without the action of the government. Wealthy people should directly help poor people. It is possible.

**Obama's G.S.**  That's a legend from the age of affluence.

**Tsuiki**  No, no.

**Obama's G.S.**  It's a legend.

**Tsuiki**  No, no, no.

**Obama's G.S.**  That's a legend. Please look at the reality now. Look at the poverty itself.

Many young people have lost their jobs and have no homes to live in. They need urgent and immediate aid from great economic power. I think that it must be the government. There's no Rockefeller of the

立木　そうです。政府抜きで、貧しい人々を、直接、助けるべきです。これは可能なことです。


オバマ守護霊　それは、豊かな時代の伝説にすぎません。


立木　いいえ、違います。

オバマ守護霊　それは伝説ですよ。

立木　そんなことはありません。

オバマ守護霊　それは伝説です。今の現実を見なさい。貧困を見てみなさい。
　多くの若者たちは、仕事をなくし、住む家もありません。だから、彼らには、巨大な経済力による、緊急かつ迅速な支援が必要なのです。その巨大な経済力とは、政府であると私は思います。20世紀のロックフェラーは、もう

## 1 Spiritual Interview with Re-elected President Obama

20$^{th}$ century. Bill Gates is not so kind to the poor, you know. (*laughs*)

**Tsuiki**  But we think we should produce many Rockefellers of the 21$^{st}$ century.

**Obama's G.S.**  That depends on their will, but it won't be in time. We must do that sacred job as soon as possible.

The government budget is enormous and we can use that in any direction. It depends on the skill of politicians and statesmen.

I want to create a peaceful world. A peaceful world doesn't require a greater military budget, so we can cut the military budget. This kind of military budget cut can be transferred to save the poor people and to cure poverty. We can create new jobs for them and pay their salaries.

This is my direction and my policy, and I won for

いないのです。ビル・ゲイツは、貧しい人々に優しくないでしょう？（笑）

立木　しかし、私たちが考えているのは、「21世紀のロックフェラーを、たくさん輩出していくべきだ」ということです。

オバマ守護霊　それは、そういう人たちの意志にかかっていますが、それでは間に合わないんですよ。われわれは、この聖なる仕事を、できるだけ早く行わなければなりません。

　政府の予算は巨大であり、われわれは、その巨大な予算をさまざまな方面に対して使うことができるのです。それは、政治家の腕にかかっています。

　私は、平和な世界をつくりたいのです。平和な世界には、これ以上の軍事予算は必要ありません。われわれは、軍事予算を削減できます。その削減した軍事予算は、貧困をなくし、貧しい人々を救済するために、転用できるのです。そして、新しい雇用を創出すれば、彼らに給料を支払うことができます。

　これが、私の目指す方向性であり、私の方針です。そ

this very reason. American people, the people of the United States, support me regarding this matter. This is the 'One America' policy.

> Note: The United States fiscal cliff refers to tax increases which will be caused by the expiration of tax cut laws, and large budget cuts will begin in 2013. As the budget will be tightened drastically, there is a chance that the economy will fall steeply like falling off of a cliff.

# 3  Politics is an Art of Words

Tsuiki   But in the Middle East…

Obama′s G.S.   Middle East?

Tsuiki   Yes, in Syria…

Obama′s G.S.   Syria? Syria, Syria.

れゆえに、私は勝利したのです。アメリカの国民、アメリカ合衆国の人々は、この点に関して、私を支持したのです。これが、「ワン・アメリカ(一つのアメリカ)政策」です。

〔注〕アメリカでは、来年（2013年）から、減税期限が切れることによる「実質的増税」と、「強制的な歳出削減」が始まる。これによって、急激な財政の引き締めが起き、崖から落ちるように景気が悪化する可能性がある。

## 3 政治とは「言葉の技術」である

立木　しかし、中東の……。

オバマ守護霊　中東？

立木　はい。シリアでは……。

オバマ守護霊　シリア？　シリアですね。

1 Spiritual Interview with Re-elected President Obama

Tsuiki   Syrian people are killed by their government and the United States doesn't…

Obama's G.S.   You want the U.S. to bomb them and kill the military force or the government?

Tsuiki   We think the United States should send forces.

Obama's G.S.   No! Jesus prohibited that. Massacre is not good. You shouldn't use money to kill people.

Tsuiki   America has the power to stop the killing.

Obama's G.S.   It's their problem. There's a reason.

立木　人々が政府によって殺害されているにもかかわらず、アメリカ合衆国は……。

オバマ守護霊　あなたは、「アメリカが爆弾でも落として、シリアの軍や政府を破壊してほしい」と考えているのですか。

立木　私たちは、「アメリカ合衆国が軍隊を送るべきだ」と考えています。

オバマ守護霊　断ります！　イエスは、それを禁じました。殺戮はよくありません。人々を殺すのにお金を使ってはならないのです。

立木　アメリカには、彼らが人々を殺すのを止める力があるのです。

オバマ守護霊　それは、彼らの問題です。彼らには、彼らなりの理由があるのです。

1 Spiritual Interview with Re-elected President Obama

**Tsuiki** But, it's also America's problem.

**Obama's G.S.** No, no. It's their problem.

They must first talk about their issues and their delegates should argue about that. They must come to a conclusion and tell them to obey the conclusion. They can argue.
That's their first step.

**Tsuiki** But, their argument went wrong…

**Obama's G.S.** The U.N. should pronounce, "Stop killing people. Stop the war."

**Tsuiki** But the government doesn't obey the order of United Nations. So, that…

**Obama's G.S.** Then, at that time, they will die. All

第1章 再選したオバマ大統領のスピリチュアル・インタビュー

立木　しかし、これはアメリカの問題でもありますよね。

オバマ守護霊　いやいや、違います。それは、彼らの問題です。

　まずは、彼らが、自分たちの問題について話し合わなければなりません。彼らの代表団が互いに議論をし、結論を出さなければならないのです。そして、その結論に従うように言わなければなりません。

　そのように、議論することが先決なのです。

立木　しかし、彼らの議論はうまくいきませんでした……。

オバマ守護霊　国連が、「人々を殺害するのをやめなさい。戦争をやめなさい」と宣言しなければならないのです。

立木　しかし、シリア政府は、国連の非難決議に従わないのですから……。

オバマ守護霊　では、そのときには、死ぬしかありませ

of them will die.

**Tsuiki**   So, America should stop the killing.

**Obama's G.S.**   It's not a matter for America.

**Tsuiki**   So, according to your policy, America may be fine, but around the world, there will be many wars.

**Obama's G.S.**   Wall?

**Tsuiki**   *Wars* and conflicts; many wars and conflicts will happen, and many people will suffer from the wars and bloodshed. Your dream of a peaceful world will not come true.

**Obama's G.S.**   OK, OK. I understand, I understand.
But for example, you first referred to the Senkaku islands; before you consider starting a war, first you

んね。みんな死ぬんですよ。

立木　だからこそ、アメリカが、シリア政権による殺害をやめさせなければならないのではないでしょうか。

オバマ守護霊　それは、アメリカの問題ではありませんよ。

立木　あなたの方針でいけば、アメリカだけはうまくいくでしょうが、世界中で「戦争（ウォー）」が頻発し……。

オバマ守護霊　なに？　「壁（ウォール）」？

立木　戦争（ウォー）、紛争（ふんそう）です。数多くの戦争が起き、数多くの人々が殺戮に苦しむことになります。そうなると、あなたの夢であるところの「平和な世界」は実現しないでしょう。

オバマ守護霊　オーケー、オーケー、分かりました。
　しかし、あなたは、例えば、最初に「尖閣諸島（せんかく）」について言及（げんきゅう）しましたが、戦争を始めることを考える前に、中国

should talk with China. You need diplomacy. That comes first. Diplomacy comes first.

Secondly, government politics needs to make some conditions to stop the conflict; for example, you can compromise with them in the economic sense or in another way.

And thirdly, you must make military action with only the Japanese or with the United States. This is the third stage.

First, diplomacy is essential.

The problem with the Japanese people is the lack of skill in diplomacy. Diplomacy depends on words. Japanese diplomats should use effective words which can persuade the Chinese people. I am constantly irritated about that.

You, Japanese people, usually use vague words and your intentions are very difficult to understand. You are wasting time.

You should change first. Please speak reasonably

第1章　再選したオバマ大統領のスピリチュアル・インタビュー

と話し合うべきです。そのためには、「外交」が必要です。それを第一にすべきです。最初にすべきことは「外交」なのです。

二番目に、政治的駆け引きによって、「紛争を止めるための条件」を整える必要があります。例えば、経済的手段、その他の方法によって、妥協点を探ることは可能です。

そして、日本単独か、あるいは、アメリカと共に軍事的行動をとるべきです。しかし、これは三番目でなければなりません。三段階目の手段なんですね。

まずは「外交」が最重要なのです。

日本人の問題点は、外交技術に欠けることです。外交は、「言葉」にかかっています。日本の外交官は、中国人を説得できるだけの効果的な言葉を使わなければなりません。そのことに関し、私は、常にイライラしています。

あなたがた日本人は、普段から曖昧な言葉しか使わず、何を言いたいのかが非常に分かりづらいため、時間を無駄にしてしまいます。

あなたがたが、まず変わらなければなりません。もっと、

and practically, and make efforts to get a clear conclusion or to acquire an effective result.

This is the direction of your diplomacy. I think that nuclear bombs or missiles are the third, fourth or fifth stage.

**Tsuiki**  I understand your opinions.

**Obama's G.S.**  For example, your words are not so effective. (*audience laughs*)

**Tsuiki**  But, diplomacy is affected by military power.

**Obama's G.S.**  No, no. That depends.

**Tsuiki**  No, no…

**Obama's G.S.**  If your speech is great and can persuade Chinese people and move them, they will follow you.

第1章　再選したオバマ大統領のスピリチュアル・インタビュー

論理的・具体的に話してください。そして、明快な結論、効果的な結果を得られるように努めてほしいのです。

　それが、あなたがたの向かうべき外交の方向であると、私は思いますね。核爆弾、核ミサイルについて考えるのは、三番目か四番目、五番目のことだと思いますよ。

立木　あなたのお考えは理解できるのですが……。

オバマ守護霊　例えば、あなたの言葉は効果的ではありません（会場笑）。

立木　しかし、外交は、軍事力によって左右されるものです。

オバマ守護霊　いやいや、違います。それは場合によるのです。

立木　いえ、いえ……。

オバマ守護霊　もし、あなたの言論が素晴らしく、中国人を説得したり、感動させたりすることができれば、彼

1 Spiritual Interview with Re-elected President Obama

A good one-hour speech is equal to a nuclear bomb.

Tsuiki   I wish you would persuade the Chinese people.

Obama´s G.S.   I will. I will, of course. I will.

Tsuiki   Yes, yes. Thank you. They don't…

Obama´s G.S.   I'm the American President. If I want to take military action and want to start a war, I can start it immediately.

But, I don't desire to do so because we have words.

We can persuade them. We can stop their actions.

If they do excessive deeds, for example, if they attacked Okinawa or other parts of Japan, I won't

第1章　再選したオバマ大統領のスピリチュアル・インタビュー

らもあなたに従いますよ。

「1時間のよいスピーチ」は、核爆弾に匹敵(ひってき)するのです。


立木　あなたに、中国人の説得をお願いしたいものです。



オバマ守護霊　やります、やります。もちろん、やりますとも。


立木　ええ。よろしくお願いします。彼らは……。


オバマ守護霊　私はアメリカ大統領ですからね。私が、「戦争を始めたい」と思い、軍事行動をとろうとすれば、すぐにでも開始できるんですよ。

　しかし、私には、そうするつもりはありません。私たちには「言葉」があるからです。

　われわれは、彼らを説得することができます。彼らの行動を止めることができるのです。

　もし、中国人の行動が行きすぎた場合、例えば、彼らが、沖縄(おきなわ)や、日本の他の地域を攻撃(こうげき)した場合には、もちろん、

## 1 Spiritual Interview with Re-elected President Obama

forgive them, of course.

If I, the American President, declare at the White House, "We will not allow China to attack Japan again!" If I say this, they can do nothing. That's all.

**Tsuiki**  Yes, yes, because you have great power, nuclear power.

**Obama's G.S.**  Yeah, of course. So, Japan should assist us.

**Tsuiki**  Yes, we have an alliance, so we…

**Obama's G.S.**  If you are going to use the word *alliance*, please persuade the local Japanese people. They are protesting against American military forces.

**Tsuiki**  Yes, that is my intention.

**Obama's G.S.**  It's a problem. Our problem.

われわれは許しません。
　私が、アメリカ大統領として、「今度、中国が日本を攻撃したら、われわれは許さない」とホワイトハウスで宣言すれば、彼らは何もできなくなります。それで終わりです。

立木　ええ。あなたには、「核兵器」という大きな力がありますからね。

オバマ守護霊　もちろん、そうです。だから、日本の側も、われわれを支援すべきなんですよ。

立木　はい、私たちは同盟国ですから……。

オバマ守護霊　「同盟国」という言葉を使うなら、地方の日本人を説得してくださいよ。彼らは、アメリカの軍隊に反対しているのですから。

立木　ええ、説得するつもりです。

オバマ守護霊　あれは問題です。われわれにとって問題

**Tsuiki**  Yes, yes. I want to persuade…

**Obama's G.S.**  Please persuade the Okinawa people.

**Tsuiki**  Yes, I want to do so and…

**Obama's G.S.**  We don't want to stay in Okinawa. We don't want to use our military budget to protect Okinawa. We don't need to and we don't want to protect Okinawa.

We have no plans to protect Okinawa, but we just want to obey the U.S.-Japan military alliance. That is our duty. So, we are doing our duty.

But, why should we do this? You, Japanese people, have not persuaded the Okinawa people enough. Even the prime minister of Japan cannot persuade them. It is the first thing.

**立木** はい。私も説得したいと思います。

**オバマ守護霊** 沖縄の人々を説得してくださいよ。

**立木** はい、そうしたいと思います。そして……。

**オバマ守護霊** 本当のことを言えば、私たちは、沖縄に米軍を駐留させたくないんですよ。沖縄を守るために、軍事予算を使いたくはないのです。そんなことをする必要はないし、したくもないのです。

　われわれに、「沖縄を守る」つもりなどないのですが、あくまで、「日米安保条約」に従っているだけなのです。それは、われわれの義務ですからね。その義務を果たしているわけです。

　しかし、なぜ、われわれが沖縄を守らなければならないのでしょうか。というのも、あなたがた日本人は、沖縄の人々を十分に説得できていません。日本の首相でさえ、彼らを説得できていないではありませんか。まずは、

If you cannot persuade Japanese people, you won't be able to persuade Chinese people either, of course. I think that is so.

**Tsuiki**  I understand.

**Obama's G.S.**  Politics is an art of words.

**Tsuiki**  Thank you for your advice.

# 4  A Vision of America Becoming a Superpower Again

**Sakakibara**  Hello, Mr. President. Let me first introduce myself. I am…

**Obama's G.S.**  Charlie. (Sakakibara's nickname)

**Sakakibara**  Yes, that's right. (*audience laughs*) How do

それが先決です。

　日本人を説得できないのなら、当然、中国人だって説得できませんよ。私はそう思いますね。


立木　分かりました。

オバマ守護霊　政治とは、「言葉の技術」なのです。

立木　アドバイスをありがとうございます。

## 4　アメリカを再び超大国にするための構想

榊原　大統領、こんにちは。まず、自己紹介をさせてください。私は……。

オバマ守護霊　"チャーリー"（榊原の愛称）だね。

榊原　はい、そうです（会場笑）。なぜご存じなのですか？

1 Spiritual Interview with Re-elected President Obama

you know my name?

**Obama's G.S.** I can just read your name in your heart.

**Sakakibara** My heart? Thank you.

I'm very honored to speak to you today. First, I would like to congratulate you for your presidency.

**Obama's G.S.** Thank you.

**Sakakibara** I have prepared several questions for you. Japanese people are very hopeful about your new presidency to create a Strong America.

**Obama's G.S.** Really? Really?

**Sakakibara** Yes, of course.

Do you know the statistics of the website supporting you? People around the world expect you to create a new world and lead the new world.

第1章　再選したオバマ大統領のスピリチュアル・インタビュー

オバマ守護霊　あなたの心を読んだだけですよ。

榊原　私の心を？　そうですか。ありがとうございます。
　今日は、あなたとお話しする機会を頂き、非常に光栄です。まずは、大統領当選、おめでとうございます。

オバマ守護霊　ありがとう。

榊原　質問をいくつか準備してきました。日本人は、あなたのこれからの任期中に、「強いアメリカ」が実現されることを非常に期待しています。

オバマ守護霊　それは本当ですか？　本当に？

榊原　ええ、もちろんです。
　あなたはご存じでしょうか。ウェブ上の統計データでは、世界中の人々があなたを支持していました。世界の人々は、「オバマ大統領が、新しい世界をつくってくれる

So, for your new presidency, could you tell us about your new design for America?

Obama's G.S.　Design?

Sakakibara　What do you want to do?

Obama's G.S.　Firstly, the unemployment rate is an essential matter.

Sakakibara　Yes.

Obama's G.S.　I want to minimize the unemployment rate. This is my first action.

Sakakibara　Yes, it's a lasting problem. It's a lasting problem for your current presidency. But it doesn't seem

のではないか。新しい世界に導いてくれるのではないか」と期待しています。

　そこで、あなたがアメリカ大統領の新たな任期を務めるに当たり、どのような国家構想を描いているかをお教えいただけますでしょうか。

オバマ守護霊　構想ですか？

榊原　何をしたいと思っておられますか？

オバマ守護霊　まずは、失業率の問題が重要事項ですね。

榊原　はい。

オバマ守護霊　「失業率を最小限にしたい」ということ、これが、私が最初に行いたいことです。

榊原　ええ、その問題は長引いていますね。現任期において、これがいまだに改善されていない点については、

to have improved yet, so what do you think of that?

Obama's G.S.　I want to use a lot of budget to create many jobs. We can hire more than one million people, especially younger and weaker people. First, producing one million jobs by next March is essential, I think.

After that, we will reconstruct our energy-creating industry…

Sakakibara　You mean the Green New Deal will continue?

Obama's G.S.　Yeah, yeah. I don't have enough success in that field, so I will re-challenge myself in creating green energy.

It is also predicted that in the U.S. there is oil shale (oil can be extracted by crushing and dry distilling the oil shale), also. I'll check it. If we have a lot of oil shale, we won't have much trouble with Middle Eastern

どう思われていますか。

**オバマ守護霊** 多くの雇用(こよう)を創出するために、多額の予算を使いたいと思っています。そうすれば、100万人以上の雇用、特に、若者や弱者を雇(やと)うことができるようになります。まずは、「来年3月までに、100万人の雇用を生み出すこと」が重要だと思っています。

　その後、エネルギー産業を再建し……。


**榊原** それは、「グリーン・ニューディール政策を続ける」ということですか？

**オバマ守護霊** そうです。あの分野においては、十分な成功をしていないので、もう一度チャレンジし、グリーン・エネルギーをつくっていきたいと思っています。

　また、「アメリカにはオイルシェールがある(地中の油母頁岩(ゆぼけつがん)を砕(くだ)いて乾留(かんりゅう)すると石油が得られる)」とも言われているので、それも調べたいですね。オイルシェールが豊富にあれば、それほど中東と揉(も)めることなく、エネ

countries and we can solve our energy problem.

Then, it will be very easy for us to create new jobs, make people affluent and regain American power.

Sakakibara   I see. You declared those policies for your current presidency, but they haven't been realized yet. How will you persuade American people about what you can do for your next presidency?

Obama's G.S.   In short, what is your point?

Sakakibara   My point is that people think that you couldn't realize your policies in your current presidency. How can you say that you can do it in your next term as President?

Obama's G.S.   Your Filipino English is a little difficult to hear, so I'm not following you, but I'll do my best, OK? (Sakakibara used to be the branch minister of the Philippines.)

ギー問題を解決できますからね。

　そうすれば、簡単に新しい雇用を生み出し、人々を豊かにして、アメリカの国力を盛り返せるでしょう。

榊原　そうですか。しかし、現任期において、あなたが最初に掲げた政策は、まだ実現できていないように思います。そこで、「次の任期で何ができるか」ということを、国民に対し、どのように説得するおつもりでしょうか？

オバマ守護霊　要するに、何が言いたいのですか。

榊原　つまり、人々は、「オバマ大統領が掲げた政策は実現できなかった」と思っています。それにもかかわらず、どうして、「次の任期では実現可能だ」と言えるのでしょうか。

オバマ守護霊　あなたのフィリピン訛りの英語は、少し聞きづらいので、十分に分かりかねますが、ベストを尽くしますよ。いいですか？（榊原は元フィリピン支部長）

**Sakakibara**  Sorry.

**Obama's G.S.**  We have a lot of people who belong to many religions and who come from various nations. It is the strong and weak point of the U.S., of course. So firstly, I must gather their powers for one purpose.

One purpose is to make the U.S. rebound and make it become a superpower again. It's my most important policy.

We can do this, I think, if we gather our powers from different nationalities, different languages, and different races. We consist of such variety of people, but there is only one America. And the 'One America' policy will save this country.

They can. They have powers to recreate this country to become greater and greater.

The glory of God will appear in this world again, and America should again be the leader of the world.

第1章　再選したオバマ大統領のスピリチュアル・インタビュー

榊原　すみません。

オバマ守護霊　アメリカには、さまざまな国から来た、さまざまな宗教に属する人々がたくさんいます。それが、アメリカの強みでもあり、当然、弱みでもあります。だから、まず、一つの目的のために、彼らの力を集めなければなりません。

　一つの目的とは、アメリカを再生させ、もう一度、超大国にすることです。それが、私の最も重要な方針です。

　そして、それは「できる」と思っています。異なった国籍・言語・人種の力を集めれば可能であると思います。われわれの国は、そのような異なった人々で成り立っていますが、アメリカは一つなのです。「一つのアメリカ」政策が、この国を救うのです。
　彼らにはできます。彼らは、この国を素晴らしくつくり変える力を持っています。
　神の栄光は、再び、この世に現れ、アメリカは、再び、世界のリーダーとならなければならない。私の任期中に、

## 1 Spiritual Interview with Re-elected President Obama

I will make the foundation of America's prosperity for the next one hundred years through my Presidency, so please rely on me.

Tsuiki   But the stock market has declined more than $300 yesterday.

Obama's G.S.   You think too small.

Tsuiki   No, no, no. Investors don't expect much from you.

Obama's G.S.   They are too afraid of the tax policy of the new presidency. They are afraid that I will make a great burden on them and their activities and performance will go down. They predict that this will happen. But I think it's just a miserable, bad nightmare. Please rely on me.

I will gather the powers of this country. We have hidden power in this country.

第1章　再選したオバマ大統領のスピリチュアル・インタビュー

今後百年にわたるアメリカの繁栄の基礎をつくろうと思っています。だから、私を信頼してください。


立木　しかし、株式市場は昨日、300ドル以上下がりました。

オバマ守護霊　あなたの考えは小さいですね。

立木　いいえ、そういうことではなく、投資家たちは、あなたの能力に期待していないのです。

オバマ守護霊　彼らは、新しい任期における税金政策について、不安を感じすぎています。「オバマの政策が、自分たちに大きな負担をかける結果、生産活動や成果が下がるのではないか」と心配しています。彼らは、そう予想しているのです。しかし、それは、単なる惨めな悪夢にすぎませんよ。どうか、私を頼りにしてほしいのです。
　私は、この国の力を結集させようと思っています。この国には、秘められた力があるのです。

For example, Hispanic people, black people, other minorities, or the people from Japan, Africa, China, South America, or other countries. If these people are given enough economic training, they can be a greater power for the new industries and future industries. Please believe and trust that.

I am relying on the power of education. They don't have enough chances to get an education. I will give them enough education so they can become greater people. I think that this kind of great people will lead America next.

**Tsuiki**　Yes, in the long run, education is a very effective way to make a country rich. But in the short term, the tax and fiscal problems are very important.

How will you persuade the Republicans of Congress?

**Obama′s G.S.**　I want to put a greater tax on Mitt Romney and get a lot of money from him. (*laughs*)

例えば、ヒスパニック系、黒人、その他の少数民族、日本やアフリカ、中国、南米、その他の国から来た人々がいます。そのような人々が十分な経済的訓練を受ければ、彼らは新しい産業や未来産業を生み出す力となります。そのことを信頼してほしいのです。

　私は、「教育の力」を信じています。彼らには、教育のチャンスが十分になかったのです。私は、彼らに十分な教育を施ほどこし、素晴らしい人材にするつもりです。そのような素晴らしい人々が、次のアメリカを導くと考えています。


立木　そうですね。長期的に見れば、教育は、国を富ませる上で、非常に効果的な方法です。しかし、短期的には、税金や財政問題が非常に重要であると思います。
　そこで、あなたは、議会の共和党議員を、どのように説得するおつもりなのでしょうか。

オバマ守護霊　ミット・ロムニーには、高い税金をかけて、多くのお金を取りたいですね（笑）。

**Tsuiki**  But they oppose your policy and your opinions.

**Obama´s G.S.**  Hahaha. But some kind of people earn too much and that money is not used in a good way, so I will teach them how to use money. I'm a teacher of the American people, so wealthy people need to be taught how to use their money. I won't take money from them. I will just teach them how to use money. Sometimes I will use the money in place of them. I will be in charge of using money.

## 5  Obama Aims to Create a "Japanese-Type Socialism" That Has a Big Middle-Class

**Tsuiki**  But such thinking is socialism.

立木　しかし、彼らは、あなたの政策、あなたのご意見に反対するでしょう。

オバマ守護霊　ハハハ。ただ、一定の人々は、稼ぎすぎている上に、そのお金は、上手に使われていません。だから、私は、彼らに、お金の使い方を教えたいと思っています。私は、アメリカ人の教師です。富裕層の人々は、お金の使い方に関して、（私から）教えを受けなければなりません。私には、彼らからお金を奪うつもりはありません。ただ、お金の使い方を教えるだけです。そして、ときには、彼らに代わって、そのお金を使うでしょう。お金を使うのが、私の役目なのです。

## 5　目指しているのは、中流階級の多い"日本型の社会主義"

立木　しかし、それは、社会主義的な考えですよね？

1 Spiritual Interview with Re-elected President Obama

**Obama's G.S.**  Socialism? No, no, no, no.

**Tsuiki**  It's a kind of socialism.

**Obama's G.S.**  Socialism? What kind of socialism do you mean?

**Tsuiki**  Everything is decided by the government. The government decides how the money is used. This is your thinking.

**Obama's G.S.**  So you are a disciple of Mitt Romney, right?

**Tsuiki**  I agree with Mitt Romney on this point.

**Obama's G.S.**  You are friends with Mormons?

**Tsuiki**  No, no, that's not what I meant.

**オバマ守護霊** 社会主義？ いやいや、違います。

**立木** 一種の社会主義ですよ。

**オバマ守護霊** 社会主義？ あなたの言われる社会主義とは、どのような意味のものですか。

**立木** 要するに、「すべてが政府によって決められる」ということです。政府によってお金の使い方が決められる。これがあなたの考え方です。

**オバマ守護霊** つまり、あなたは、「ミット・ロムニーの弟子」ということですか。

**立木** この点について、私は、ミット・ロムニーの考えに賛成です。

**オバマ守護霊** あなたは、モルモン教徒の友人なのですか。

**立木** いえいえ。別に、そういうわけではありません。

1 Spiritual Interview with Re-elected President Obama

Obama's G.S.　OK, OK, I understand.

Tsuiki　I don't see Mormons as my enemies.

Obama's G.S.　Uh-huh, OK.

Socialism has a lot of faces. For example, one is where there is a big government and very poor people only. This is one kind of socialism. A small number of people are leaders and others are very poor and have no political power. This is one style of socialism.

But the next stage of socialism is that the middle power becomes very strong. This is the Japanese type of socialism. This type has a strong middle power but, in addition to that, the upper-class can be active and the upper-class people take charge of the sacred responsibility, instead of God. They should do their crusade and give their money to the lower-class.

This is one kind of socialism, but it's not the

第1章　再選したオバマ大統領のスピリチュアル・インタビュー

オバマ守護霊　そうか、そうか。分かりましたよ。

立木　ただ、私は、モルモン教徒を敵だとは思っていません。

オバマ守護霊　分かりました。
　社会主義には、さまざまな面があります。例えば、一つは、大きな政府の下、非常に貧しい人々だけがいる状態です。これが社会主義の一側面です。「一握りの人だけが指導者であり、他の人々は非常に貧しく、何の政治力も持っていない」というのが、社会主義の一つのスタイルです。
　しかし、社会主義の次のステージは、中流階級が大きな力を持っている状態です。これは、日本型の社会主義ですね。このタイプでは、中流階級が強い上に、上流階級も活発で、上流階級の人々が、神の代わりに聖なる責任を果たしている状態です。すなわち、彼らは、貧しさを撲滅するために戦い、底辺層の人々にお金を注ぎ込まなくてはならないわけです。
　これも、ある種の社会主義のかたちですが、それほど

unfortunate kind of socialism.

I think the Japanese system is not so bad. The Japanese system has many middle-class people. This is very good.

In America, 1% of the people have a big share of America's money. It's too excessive. Government should rearrange the percentage so that it's like the Japanese style.

In Japan, there are very few people who earn more than 1 million dollars. So we, America, should restrain ourselves.

For example, in a large company, if you become the chairman or President of that large company, in Japan, you earn five thousand million yen when you retire. But I don't think that it's good. They don't work so much. They have a lot of employees and that is the reason for them to earn such large amounts of money.

So they should restrain themselves and return some part of the earnings to other employees who are very poor. If they restrain themselves, that company can

不幸な形態ではないと思うのです。

　私は、「日本のシステムは悪くない」と思っています。日本のシステムでは、中流階級が多いのですが、それは非常によいことです。

　アメリカでは、1パーセントの人々がアメリカの大部分の富を持っていますが、それは行きすぎです。政府が、日本のスタイルのような割合になるように、再調整しなければなりません。

　日本では、100万ドル以上稼ぐ人は非常に少ないのです。だから、われわれアメリカも、稼ぎすぎを慎まなければなりません。

　例えば、大企業の会長や社長になれば、日本円で50億もの退職金がもらえます。しかし、それはよいことではないと思いますね。彼らは、そんなに働いていません。従業員が大勢いるからこそ、そのような巨額の富を稼げるのです。


　だから、彼らは慎まなければなりません。そして、稼ぎの一部を、他の貧しい従業員に還元しなければなりません。彼らがもっと慎めば、その企業はさらに多くの人

hire more people, jobless people, as workers.

So people are made by God equally. You may say that there should be equality of chance and not equality of result. But the equality of result sometimes makes the equality of chances to challenge yourself for a new start of your lives.

For example, if you have billions of dollars when you are at the age of three or five, like the Hatoyama family of Japan, it is easier for you to get a good education and great job. If a mother gave a lot of pocket money, more than the American President's income, to her sons, it's not fair.

So socialism itself is not so bad. The equality of result is sometimes the equality of chance, so don't misunderstand that.

You understand what I am saying?

Tsuiki   Yes, but socialism…

を雇うことができます。失業している人々を、従業員として雇うこともできるのです。

　人はみな神によって平等に創られています。あなたがたは、おそらく、「その平等とは、結果の平等ではなく、チャンスの平等だ」と言うのでしょう。しかし、結果の平等は、ときとして、人生において新しいスタートを切るためにチャレンジするチャンスを、平等に与えてくれるものなのです。

　例えば、三歳や五歳のときに、何十億円ものお金があれば、よい教育を受けて、素晴らしい仕事に就くことが容易にできるでしょう。日本の鳩山一家がそうですね。しかし、母親が、アメリカ大統領の収入以上に巨額な富を息子に小遣いとして与えることは、公平ではないと思います。

　社会主義自体は、それほど悪いものではありません。結果の平等は、ときとして、チャンスの平等になりますので、それを誤解してはいけないのです。

　言っていることが分かりますか。

立木　はい。しかし、社会主義は……。

1 Spiritual Interview with Re-elected President Obama

**Obama's G.S.**  If you were Hatoyama*, and you are the party leader of the Happiness Realization Party, then you can be a lawmaker and you can be the prime minister of Japan. You can accomplish that ten years or twenty years earlier than as scheduled. Is this fair?

**Tsuiki**  But socialism often develops into totalitarianism from the arbitrary thinking of political leaders. So it's very dangerous.

**Obama's G.S.**  The name of the system is not so essential. For example, China is communist. But, the prime minister earns a hundred times more than I earn a year. It is not so fair. Communism is more forceful than socialism in its name, but in reality, it is not like this.

So, the name of the system is not so important. The reality is important. The reality is how many people you can make happier, wealthier, feel not so poor, or feel not so impoverished. This is essential. This is a

---

* Yukio Hatoyama is a Japanese politician who served as Japan's prime minister from September 16, 2009 to June 8, 2010. He is from a distinguished political and industrial family.

**オバマ守護霊** もし、あなたが鳩山氏で、しかも、幸福実現党の党首だったなら、あなたは国会議員になって、予定より十年も二十年も早く、日本の首相になれますよ。それが公平ですか。

**立木** ただ、社会主義は、政治指導者の恣意的な考えによって全体主義になることもあり、非常に危険だと思います。

**オバマ守護霊** 制度の名前は、そんなに重要ではありません。例えば、中国は共産主義です。しかし、そこの首相は、年間で、私の何百倍以上も稼いでいます。それは、あまり公平なことではありません。共産主義は、言葉の上では、社会主義より強制力がありますが、現実はそうではないのです。

 したがって、制度の名前はそれほど重要ではありません。重要なのは現実です。その現実とは、「何人の人々を、より幸福に、より豊かにできたか。貧しさを感じさせなかったか」ということです。それが重要です。それは政

matter of politics.

If jobless people are living around Manhattan or other cities, you must save them. It's the first job of politicians. So there is no socialism. There is no capitalism. There is no market-oriented liberalism. There is no communism. We must just seek for the happy future of more and more people. That is the only aim for lawmakers and politicians.

# 6 Which One First: Educating the Poor or Creating a New Industry?

**Tsuiki**　Yes, I understand it. But your policy to hike taxes on the wealthy will discourage people from working hard and becoming successful. This would lead to the decline of American economy?

**Obama's G.S.**　No, no. That is not true. I used to work, in Chicago, for the poor people. There are a lot of poor people there. Such kind of poor people

治の問題です。

　もし、マンハッタンやその他の都市に、失業者が多くいるのなら、彼らを救わなければなりません。それは、政治家がまずやらなければならない仕事です。だから、社会主義も、資本主義もありません。市場指向型自由主義も、共産主義もありません。ただ、より多くの人々の幸せな未来を追求するだけですよ。それこそが、政治家や国会議員の唯一の目的なのです。

## 6 「貧困層の教育」が先か、「新産業の創造」が先か

立木　それは分かります。しかし、「富裕層に対する税金を上げる」という、あなたの政策は、一生懸命働いて成功しようという人々のやる気を削ぎます。その結果、アメリカ経済は衰退するのではないでしょうか。

オバマ守護霊　いやいや、それは違います。私は、シカゴで貧しい人々のために働いていました。そこには貧しい人々が大勢いましたよ。彼らには子供がいますが、当然、

have poor children, of course, and such kind of poor children cannot get higher education, and if they cannot get higher education, they cannot make a lot of money. I don't think that this is a good situation.

So if the jobless people or, although it is difficult to make the line, for people who earn ten percent of your income, which is just a guess, it might be difficult for that child to go to the University of Tokyo in Japan. But if that child can get financial support, they can get enough education. They can be a new greater power for the industry; they can be doctors, executives, or take on other jobs.

I am supporting the poor people, but my aim is to educate them, so they can reach the middle level. I think it's also the desire of God.

However, the richer people or the richest people don't care about the poor people. They can do everything. If they don't like America, they can go to Singapore, Canada, or anywhere else in the world. They can even go to the universe and another planet.

その子供たちも貧しいので、高い教育は受けられません。高い教育を受けられなければ、多くのお金を稼ぐことはできないわけです。それは、あまり歓迎されることではないと思います。

　失業者等と同じ線上で考えるのは難しいかもしれませんが、例えば、日本であっても、あなたの収入の10パーセントしか稼いでいない人は、単なる推測にすぎませんが、おそらく、子供を東京大学に行かせることは難しいでしょう。しかし、金銭的な援助があれば、彼らもよい教育を受けることができ、産業界の新しい力となれます。医者や経営者などにもなれるわけです。


　私は、貧しい人を支援しています。その目的は、彼らを教育して、彼らの能力を中流階級まで引き上げることです。私は、それも神の願いだと思っています。

　しかし、裕福な人や最富裕層は、貧しい人々のことを気にとめません。富裕層の人々は何でもできます。もし、彼らがアメリカを嫌うなら、シンガポールなり、カナダなり、世界のどこにでも行けばよいのです。宇宙や他の惑星にさえ行けるでしょう。そうすればよいのです。何

It's OK for them. If they pay billions of dollars, they can. So we don't need to think too much about the richest people. Just…

Sakakibara   If that can be allowed, the American economy will decline. What do you think?

Obama's G.S.   So, don't make great conflicts regarding the Senkaku islands or the Takeshima islands. Don't fight against China and Korea. We need more military budget regarding that matter. So please keep our money for our poor people. I ask you.

Sakakibara   As you know, Happy Science suggests that to expand the economy, we should create a new business. New businesses will expand the new economy. That's the basic knowledge of economic growth. But if you take money from the rich people, they will not have the money to invest in the new business.

第1章　再選したオバマ大統領のスピリチュアル・インタビュー

十億円か支払えば可能でしょうからね。だから、富裕層の人々については、あまり考えてはいません。ただ……。

榊原　もし、それを許せば、アメリカ経済は衰退するでしょう。それについては、どう思われますか。

オバマ守護霊　だから、尖閣諸島や竹島のことで、大きな争いを起こしてはいけません。中国や韓国と戦わないでください。この問題に関して、われわれの軍事予算がもっと必要になってしまいます。貧しい国民のために予算を確保させてください。私から君へのお願いです。

榊原　ご存じのとおり、幸福の科学では、「経済成長のためには、新規事業を創造すべきだ」と提案しています。新規事業が経済を拡大させます。それが、私たちの提言している経済成長の基本的な考え方です。しかし、お金持ちからお金を奪うと、彼らは新規事業に資金を投資しなくなるでしょう。

## 1 Spiritual Interview with Re-elected President Obama

**Obama's G.S.** Before creating new businesses, you need education, sufficient education. So to create sufficient education, you must collect tax money from the rich people. This tax should be spent on education and the medical care for weaker people.

**Sakakibara** You mean "Obama care."

**Obama's G.S.** Of course. I think that this is the first direction. A new industry will follow after good education.

**Sakakibara** I see. You will also use the policy, the "Green New Deal," for example.

**Obama's G.S.** Good New Deal?

**Sakakibara** Green New Deal.

**Obama's G.S.** Green New Deal.

オバマ守護霊　新規事業の前に、教育が必要です。十分な教育です。十分な教育環境をつくるために、富裕層から税金を徴収しなければなりません。そして、この税金が、教育や、弱者への医療費に使われるべきなのです。

榊原　「オバマケア」ですね。

オバマ守護霊　当然です。これが最初の方向性だと思っています。「新産業」は、「よい教育」の次に来るのです。

榊原　なるほど。そして、「グリーン・ニューディール」等の政策もとられるおつもりですね。

オバマ守護霊　グッド・ニューディール？

榊原　グリーン・ニューディールです。

オバマ守護霊　グリーン・ニューディールね。

**Sakakibara**  You will use this as a government policy. That's what I understand.

**Obama's G.S.**  It was not so successful, I admit. It was not so successful. The Green New Deal cannot produce a lot of employees. It's a small business, so I don't think it's sufficient.

**Sakakibara**  So you will look for another…

**Obama's G.S.**  Yeah, of course.

**Sakakibara**  …source of investment.

**Obama's G.S.**  Another industry is required.

**Sakakibara**  I see, I see.
 Master Okawa, as you know, is the World

榊原　あなたが、政府の政策として実施されると理解しています。

オバマ守護霊　あまりうまくいっていないことは、私も認めますよ。あまり成功していません。つまり、「グリーン・ニューディールでは、大量の雇用は生めない」ということです。小さい事業ですからね。あまり十分ではないと思います。

榊原　そうすると、別のものを探すのでしょうか。

オバマ守護霊　もちろんです。

榊原　投資先を…。

オバマ守護霊　別の産業が必要です。

榊原　分かりました。
　大川総裁は、ご存じのとおり、「ワールド・ティーチャー

Teacher...

Obama's G.S.  I don't know that.

Sakakibara  Happy Science is suggesting that you find...

Obama's G.S.  suggesting me?

Sakakibara  You will find a new frontier to enlarge businesses.

Obama's G.S.  Bad Obama?

Sakakibara  Yes, to you. As President of the United States, what do you think? About the new frontier...

Obama's G.S.  OK. I have the talent to be a religious pioneer, and Mr. Okawa has the talent to become Bill Gates; that's the conclusion.

(世界教師)」ですが……。

オバマ守護霊　知らないですね。

榊原　幸福の科学では、あなたが見つけることを提案していて……。

オバマ守護霊　私に提案しているのですか。

榊原　あなたが、事業を成長させるニューフロンティアを見つけることを（提案しているのです）。

オバマ守護霊　悪いオバマが？

榊原　あなたに、です。合衆国大統領として、どう思われますか。ニューフロンティアについて……。

オバマ守護霊　オーケー。私には、宗教的先駆者になる才能がある。大川さんには、ビル・ゲイツになる才能がある。それが結論です。

Sakakibara   Is that the point you want to make?

# 7 President Obama: The Secrets and Tendencies of His Soul

Sakakibara   Now I have another question from a spiritual perspective.

Obama's G.S.   Spiritual perspective?

Sakakibara   I read your spiritual message and you were King Montezuma II in your past life (*2012 Will the World Really End?*, by Happy Science.).

He predicted that you will trigger…

Obama's G.S.   trigger?

Sakakibara   … trigger the end of the world.

榊原　それが、あなたのおっしゃりたいことですね。

## 7　オバマ大統領の魂の秘密と傾向性

榊原　それでは、ここで、霊的観点から別の質問をさせていただきます。

オバマ守護霊　霊的観点？

榊原　私は、あなたの魂の兄弟であり、過去世である、モンテスマ２世の霊言を読みました（『2012年人類に終末は来るのか？』〔幸福の科学出版刊〕参照）。
　彼は、あなたが引き金を引くと予言していました。

オバマ守護霊　引き金？

榊原　「世界の終わり」の引き金です。

## 1 Spiritual Interview with Re-elected President Obama

Obama′s G.S.   The end?

Sakakibara   How do you feel about that? If you are re-elected as the next President…

Obama′s G.S.   I'm Protestant, you know, I'm Protestant.

Sakakibara   What do you mean by that?

Obama′s G.S.   I'm a very serious Protestant, so I don't think too much about the past life. Is that OK? Is it enough?

Sakakibara   Oh really? No, no, You said you have a trauma…

Obama′s G.S.   A trauma?

Sakakibara   …that you were insulted by…

第1章　再選したオバマ大統領のスピリチュアル・インタビュー

オバマ守護霊　終わり？

榊原　それについて、どう思われますか。もし、あなたが次期大統領に再選されれば……。

オバマ守護霊　私はプロテスタントです。君も知っているでしょう。私はプロテスタントなんですよ。

榊原　「プロテスタント」というのは、どういう意味ですか。

オバマ守護霊　私は、敬虔(けいけん)なプロテスタントなのです。だから、過去世についてはあまり考えません。それでいいでしょう？　十分ですか。

榊原　本当でしょうか。いえいえ、あなたにはトラウマがあると言われていました。

オバマ守護霊　トラウマ？

榊原　「侮辱(ぶじょく)された」と……。

1 Spiritual Interview with Re-elected President Obama

Obama's G.S.　I'm the President! Be careful of what you say.

Sakakibara　Sorry.

Obama's G.S.　I'm Mr. President. Don't use the word *trauma* so easily.

Sakakibara　Sorry. You said you had the problem of being insulted by white people in your past life.

Obama's G.S.　Now?

Sakakibara　Yes, partly now.

Obama's G.S.　White people?

Sakakibara　So you might have some grudges against white people. Is that right? Or have you changed

116

第1章　再選したオバマ大統領のスピリチュアル・インタビュー

オバマ守護霊　私は大統領ですよ！　発言には気をつけなさい。

榊原　すみません。

オバマ守護霊　私は大統領です。簡単に「トラウマ」などという言葉を使ってはいけません。

榊原　申し訳ありません。あなたは、過去世で、「白人に侮辱された」という問題を持っていたと……。

オバマ守護霊　今？

榊原　今も、部分的にはそうかもしれません。

オバマ守護霊　白人ですか。

榊原　ですから、白人に対して、恨みの感情をお持ちではないかと思うのです。そうではありませんか。あるいは、

1 Spiritual Interview with Re-elected President Obama

your mind?

Obama's G.S.　OK, OK. I will give you an answer from another angle. I, myself, am an angel, you know?

Sakakibara　Yes, I understand, yes.

Obama's G.S.　I am an angel.

Sakakibara　You (Montezuma II) said you will realize world justice by destroying white people.

Obama's G.S.　No, no. Angels don't destroy other people. I just want to save the minorities.

Sakakibara　I see and you know, Master Okawa, God of the Earth, El Cantare, suggested that you….

第1章　再選したオバマ大統領のスピリチュアル・インタビュー

気持ちが変わられましたか。

**オバマ守護霊**　分かった、分かった。あなたに別の角度から答えを付け加えましょう。私は天使なのです。分かっていますか。

**榊原**　はい。もちろん、分かります。

**オバマ守護霊**　私は天使です。

**榊原**　あなた（モンテスマ２世）は、「白人を滅ぼし、世界の正義を実現する」とおっしゃっていました。

**オバマ守護霊**　それは違います。天使は、他人を殺したりしません。そうではなく、マイノリティーの人たちを救いたいだけなのです。

**榊原**　分かりました。あなたは、大川総裁、すなわち地球神エル・カンターレがおっしゃっていることを……。

## 1 Spiritual Interview with Re-elected President Obama

Obama's G.S.   I don't know El Cantare, but I know Rient Arl Croud (King of the ancient Incan civilization. A branch spirit of El Cantare).

Sakakibara   OK, OK.

Obama's G.S.   I know, I know.

Sakakibara   Rient Arl Croud expects that you wll choose to take true world justice and create peace in the world; that's your justice as the President of the United States.

Obama's G.S.   What I want to say is that I am the next Jesus Christ. The tendency of my soul is like that of Jesus Christ. Next time, I will become Jesus Christ.

Sakakibara   So you mean to say, you don't care about this world, the earthly world?

## 第1章　再選したオバマ大統領のスピリチュアル・インタビュー

オバマ守護霊　エル・カンターレは知りません。しかし、リエント・アール・クラウド（古代インカの王。エル・カンターレの魂の分身）は知っています。

榊原　分かりました。

オバマ守護霊　知っていますよ。

榊原　リエント・アール・クラウドは、あなたが、世界の平和を実現するために、真なる「世界の正義」を選ぶことを期待されています。それは、アメリカ合衆国の大統領としての正義です。

オバマ守護霊　私は、「自分が、次のイエス・キリストなのだ」と言いたいのです。私の魂の傾向性は、私の魂は、イエス・キリストのようなものなのです。次は、私がイエス・キリストになるでしょう。

榊原　つまり、「この世の世界、地上世界はどうでもいい」ということでしょうか。

1 Spiritual Interview with Re-elected President Obama

Obama's G.S.　No. I just want to say that I'm not a self-centered person.

Sakakibara　I see.

Obama's G.S.　I want to love other people. I want to work for the profit of other people.

Sakakibara　I see. So does that include white people?

Obama's G.S.　Yeah, of course, of course.

Sakakibara　OK, I understand. It seems that you have changed your mind and you are seeking for world justice to protect the world and create world peace.

Obama's G.S.　But I also have the tendency to create peace without relying heavily on military forces. Military forces, in the long run, will kill a lot of

オバマ守護霊　いやいや、違います。私は、「自己中心的な人間ではない」と言いたいのです。

榊原　分かりました。

オバマ守護霊　私は他人を愛したいのです。他の人の利益のために働きたいのです。

榊原　そうですか。そこには、白人も含まれますか。

オバマ守護霊　もちろん、当然のことです。

榊原　分かりました。心を入れ替えて、世界の平和を守るために、正義を求めるわけですね。

オバマ守護霊　しかし、私は、「平和をつくるために、軍事力に頼りすぎない」という傾向性も持っています。軍事力は、長期的には大量の人を殺します。だから、軍事

1 Spiritual Interview with Re-elected President Obama

people. That is why we do not depend on them. We should talk about peace. We can overcome conflicting opinions. This is our first step. Be peaceful, Mr. Tsuiki.

Tsuiki　But, I feel that not using military power is the cause of many deaths in Syria. So…

Obama's G.S.　If they run out of money, they will stop the war. To continue a war, they need money. If they don't have enough money, they will stop.

If the United States intervened, the Chinese government will assist them. They will provide monetary aid to the Syrian government and it will lead to America using military power to protect the civilians. Then, there will be more disasters.

So, they should talk, instead of killing each other. They belong to the same nation, so I think they can talk. In the old times, Syrians were Christians and now they are Islamic people, but fundamentally

力には頼りません。私たちは平和について話し合うべきです。そうすれば、意見の対立を乗り越えられます。それが最初にあるべきです。立木さん、平和的になりなさい。

**立木** しかし、私は、「軍事力を使用しないことが、シリアでの大量殺戮の原因になっている」と思います。ですから……。

**オバマ守護霊** 彼らは資金がなくなれば、戦争をやめます。彼らは戦争をやめるでしょう。戦争をするには、お金が必要です。十分な資金がなくなれば、やめるはずです。

　もし、アメリカが介入すれば、中国が力を貸すでしょう。つまり、「中国政府が、シリア政府に資金援助を行う」ということです。そうなると、アメリカは、市民を守るために軍事力を使うことになります。それは、さらなる被害を生むと私は予想します。

　彼らは、殺し合う代わりに、話し合うべきです。彼らは同じ国民なのだから、それは可能だと思います。シリア国民は、かつてキリスト教徒でした。今はイスラム教徒ですが、根本的にはお互いを理解できるはずです。彼

1 Spiritual Interview with Re-elected President Obama

speaking, they should be capable of understanding each other. I hope so. I think a leader is required.

Tsuiki   But you are extremely concerned about the government budget or deficit.

Obama's G.S.   OK, OK. Not having a budget is not the essential problem.

If the situation in Syria is that serious, I will declare, "Stop the war." I will say that without using a bomb. As the American President, I will say, "Stop the war." Please interpret the meaning of the order "Stop the war, just stop the war" by the American President.

Sakakibara   Now, I have a question. What will you do if China gains a military power greater than that of the United States?

Obama's G.S.   I will retire at that time. (*laughs*) At that time, the Republicans will fight against them.

## 第1章　再選したオバマ大統領のスピリチュアル・インタビュー

らがお互いに理解し合えることを私は願っています。リーダーが必要なだけだと思いますよ。

**立木**　しかし、あなたは、予算や財政赤字を非常に気にされています。

**オバマ守護霊**　分かった、分かった。予算がないことは、本質的な問題ではありません。
　シリアがそれほど深刻な状況なのであれば、私は「戦争をやめよ」と宣言するつもりです。私は、爆弾なしで、アメリカ大統領として、「戦争をやめなさい。どうか、中断してください」と言います。「とにかく戦争をやめよ」というアメリカ大統領の命令の意味を理解してください。

**榊原**　そこで、質問があります。もし、中国が軍事予算を拡大し、アメリカを超える軍事力を持ったら、どうされますか。

**オバマ守護霊**　そのころには、引退しているでしょう。ハハハハ。そのときは、共和党が戦うでしょう。

# 8 Xi Jinping is Like the Reincarnation of Mao Zedong

Ichikawa   In China, Xi Jinping will become the next leader of the Communist party.

Obama's G.S.   Xi Jinping.

Ichikawa   How do you evaluate his position, his power or his deed?

Obama's G.S.   It is very difficult to calculate his potential power, but I think he's the old-fashioned type of politician in China. He likes power. In China, there is a struggle between two or three factions. The conclusion is unpredictable.

I'm guessing Xi Jinping is not so skilled in economics. If you are looking at him from the standpoint of economics or economic profit, you will misunderstand

## 8 習近平氏は
## 「毛沢東が生まれ変わったような人物」

市川　中国では、習近平が次期共産党総書記になります。

オバマ守護霊　習近平？

市川　彼の立場や力、行動について、どう評価されますか。

オバマ守護霊　彼の潜在能力を測るのは非常に難しいでしょう。彼は、中国の古いタイプの政治家であり、権力を好むと思われます。今の中国では、二つか三つの派閥間で争いが起きていて、この結末は予測不能です。

　また、習近平は、経済があまり得意ではないと思われます。もし、あなたが、彼を、経済的利益の観点で考えるならば、誤解するでしょう。彼は"古い権力"ですから、

## 1 Spiritual Interview with Re-elected President Obama

him. There would be a misunderstanding because he is an "old power." He wants to be the next Mao Zedong, so he thinks about agriculture and nuclear weapons. So he is the old type of politician.

So Japanese people will misunderstand him. You, Japanese people, do not understand him. Japanese economic powers, I mean the companies, great companies and the industry members cannot understand him.

I don't want to use this kind of word, but I think he is like the reincarnation of Mao Zedong, so you will feel great difficulty in developing a friendly relationship with him.

**Tsuiki** Are you planning on persuading him in order to bring peace to the world?

**Obama's G.S.** Yeah, I'm thinking about that. But, if there should be a nuclear war between China and the U.S. — I don't know whether you desire that or

誤解が生じるでしょうね。彼は、"次の毛沢東"になりたいのです。だから、農業や核兵器のことを考えています。要するに、古いタイプの政治家なのです。

　日本人は彼を誤解するでしょう。今、あなたがた日本人は、彼を理解できていません。日本の経済的なパワー、すなわち大企業や産業界のメンバーは、彼を理解できません。

　こういう言い方はしたくありませんが、例えて言えば、彼は、毛沢東が生まれ変わったような人物なのです。だから、あなたがたは、彼と友好関係を結ぶことに大きな困難を感じるでしょう。

立木　あなたは、世界に平和をもたらすよう、彼を説得する意志をお持ちですか。

オバマ守護霊　そうですね。そう考えていますよ。米中の核戦争がありうるとしても──あなたがたがそれを望んでいるかどうかは知りませんが──、そのかわり、そ

## 1 Spiritual Interview with Re-elected President Obama

not — we can be friends in the economic field first, instead of getting into such a war. I'm guessing that the resurrection of the American economy depends on the friendship with China.

So I dare say to you; Japan, South Korea, China and America should be friends. If Xi Jinping takes an aggressive approach against you, I will persuade him to treat you with mercy.

**Tsuiki**   Thank you very much.

**Ichikawa**   Lastly, could you give new messages to the American people and to the world?

**Obama's G.S.**   Please rely on me. I am the new hope. I will make *One America*. One America will be the new hope of the world. One America will renew the Earth. I will make new order in terms of peace. That is my mission. Please rely on the American President.

第1章　再選したオバマ大統領のスピリチュアル・インタビュー

うなる前に、経済分野で中国と友達になることができるでしょう。アメリカ経済の復活は、中国との友好関係にかかっていると予想しています。

　だから、あえて、あなたがたに言いますが、日本と韓国、中国、アメリカは、友達になるべきです。そして、もし、習近平があなたがたに強硬な姿勢を取るならば、私は、慈悲を持って接するように彼を説得しましょう。

立木　ありがとうございました。

市川　それでは、締めくくりといたしまして、アメリカ国民と世界に向けて、新しいメッセージを頂ければ幸いです。

オバマ守護霊　私を頼りにしてください。私が新たな希望です。私が「一つのアメリカ」をつくります。「一つのアメリカ」が、世界の新たな希望になるでしょう。「一つのアメリカ」が、地球を再生させるでしょう。私は平和の意味において、新たな秩序をつくります。これが私の

133

**Ichikawa**  Thank you very much. Mr. President.

**Okawa**  (To Obama's G.S.) Thank you.

# 9 President Obama is Planning to Prioritize Education and Increase Taxes on the Wealthy

**Okawa**  He was really determined.

I'm not sure if Mr. Tsuiki's portion of the interview will actually be publishable in our book. (Turns to Tsuiki) How was it?

**Tsuiki**  It was tough.

**Okawa**  Yes, it sure was.

使命です。どうか、アメリカ大統領を信頼してください。

市川　大統領閣下、ありがとうございました。

大川隆法　（オバマ大統領の守護霊に）ありがとうございました。

## 9　教育を重視し、富裕層への増税を考えているオバマ大統領

大川隆法　力が入っていましたね。
　立木さんとの会話の部分が活字化の際に使えるかどうか、分かりませんが、（立木に）どうでしたか。

立木　大変でした。

大川隆法　ああ。大変でしたね。

1 Spiritual Interview with Re-elected President Obama

Tsuiki   There were many things that I felt were uneasy during the interview.

Okawa   Indeed. His thoughts were exactly as we expected.

Tsuiki   Yes, they were.

Okawa   President Obama used to work in the slums, so he wants to invest in the poor and educate them. By doing so, he wants to get them out of unemployment and help them find their jobs.

The guardian spirit of President Obama is thinking, "Education first. There is no way we can create new industries without first giving proper education. The creation of a new industry starts from education."

It is true that there are many people in poverty who do not have the opportunity to receive an education, especially among the minorities.

He wishes to give these people an opportunity by

第1章 再選したオバマ大統領のスピリチュアル・インタビュー

立木　ただ、彼の話の内容には、こちらが不安を感じる要素がかなりあります。

大川隆法　ええ。彼の基本的な考え方は、われわれが予想したとおりのものでしたね。

立木　はい。そうでした。

大川隆法　オバマ大統領は貧民街でも働いていたので、底辺層のところにお金を投入し、彼らを教育することによって、彼らがジョブレス（失業者）から脱し、いろいろな仕事に就けるようにしたいのです。
　彼は、「今、『ニューインダストリー（新しい産業）をつくる』と言っても、それは、まず教育から始まるのだ。教育を受けなければ、新しい産業を起こしようがないではないか」と考えています。
　確かに、教育を受けるチャンスのない、貧しい人たちがいるのは事実です。特に、マイノリティーの人たちがそうです。
　彼は、「そういう人たちにチャンスを与えたい」と考え、

increasing taxes on the wealthy to raise the necessary funds for this. This is the reason why he said the wealthy do not need to make more money than they already are, and that they should restrain themselves.

The stocks on Wall Street have dropped, but he thinks very little of it. He thinks that only a small portion of voters – the investors, who are more than wealthy – have lost just a little of their assets. That's how he thinks.

Another important point is his perspective on equality, which is a rebuttal to what we are saying.

We, Happy Science, say "Equal opportunity is important. If we seek equal results, we will make people unhappy as we head toward communism." To this, the guardian spirit of President Obama said something like, "There must be equal results to a certain degree. Otherwise, we would lose equal opportunities."

Take, for example, Wen Jiabao of China. His family possesses roughly 2.7 billion USD. There is no equality of opportunities between a person who

第1章　再選したオバマ大統領のスピリチュアル・インタビュー

そのためのお金を富裕層への増税で賄おうとしています。だから、「富裕層は、もう、そんなに儲けなくてもよいだろう。少しぐらいは自制してもよいのではないか」というようなことを言っているわけですね。

だから、ウォールストリートで株価が下がったのですが、それについて、彼は、「アメリカの全有権者から見れば、この株価の下落で損をした人たちは一部であり、投資家という、お金が余っている大金持ちたちの資産が少し減っただけだ」と考えて、別に何とも思っていないのです。

もう一つのポイントは、平等に関する彼の見解です。これは、当会が言っていることに対する反論でもあるでしょう。

当会は、「チャンスの平等が大事である。結果の平等を求めすぎると、いわゆる共産主義に陥り、人々は不幸になる」という言い方をしているのですが、彼は、「ある程度、結果の平等もなければ、チャンスの平等がなくなることもある」というように言っていました。

例えば、「中国の温家宝の一族のように、約2200億円も貯めている人たちのところに生まれた人と、月に1万円しか収入がない家に生まれた人とでは、チャンスの平

was born in that family and a person who was born in a family with a monthly income of only 120 USD (10,000 JPY). That is what he means.

Therefore, he thinks there shouldn't be such a wide gap between the rich and the poor because equal results can lead to equal opportunities. To avoid creating too wide of a gap, the wealthy must restrain themselves. This is what he is thinking.

He also said that Mr. Tsuiki wouldn't have been able to attend the University of Tokyo if his parents earned only one tenth of what they did.

**Tsuiki** Yes, he said so.

**Okawa** That may be true. (*laughs*)

**Tsuiki** Yes. But I think charities and donations should be applied to education, rather than authorities collecting taxes and designating that to education. I think it's a bit of a risky idea to fund everything with

第1章　再選したオバマ大統領のスピリチュアル・インタビュー

等があるはずはないでしょう」ということですね。


　だから、「結果の平等には、ある程度、チャンスの平等につながる面もあるので、あまりにも差が開きすぎてはいけない。そうならないよう、富裕層は少し自制しなければいけないのではないか」と考えているわけです。

　「立木さんだって、家の収入が10分の1だったら、東大には行けなかったでしょう」と……。


立木　はい。そのように言われました。

大川隆法　そうかもしれませんね（笑）。

立木　はい。ただ、税金というかたちで権力によってお金を集め、それを教育に充てるのではなく、「ボランティア的なマネーが教育のほうに回るようにする」という方法があると思うのです。「何でも税金で取ろう」という考

taxes.

# 10 President Obama Will Need to Consider GOP's Opinions Under the "Divided Congress"

Okawa    President Obama won this election by a slim margin, owing to the support from the young people in unemployment, African-Americans and Hispanics.

The destruction caused by Hurricane Sandy actually turned out in his favor. He put his campaign on hold and worked to resolve the problems. Mr. Romney, on the other hand, was aiming for a small government, and that is why he lost.

He said that the money used by FEMA (Federal Emergency Management Agency) was a waste, that there is no need for such an agency and that each individual should resolve on their own.

However, many people thought, "Rich people may be capable of doing so, but the poor cannot.

え方は少し危険ではないでしょうか。

## 10 「ねじれ議会」の下では、ある程度、共和党に配慮せざるをえない

大川隆法　オバマ大統領は、今回の大統領選では、失業中の若者、黒人、ヒスパニック系の人たちの支持を受け、かろうじて僅差で勝っています。

　それと、彼には、アメリカを襲ったハリケーンが幸いしたようです。彼は、選挙運動を中止し、災害対策の陣頭指揮を執りましたが、「小さな政府」を訴えていたロムニー氏は、あれで敗れたのです。

　ロムニー氏は、「緊急事態管理庁で使われているお金は無駄だ。ああいう役所は要らない。各自が自分で対応すればよいのだ」というようなことを言っていました。

　しかし、「それは、お金持ちにならできるだろうが、貧乏人にはできない。ああいうハリケーンが来て、被害が

1 Spiritual Interview with Re-elected President Obama

Hurricane Sandy did a lot of damage to us. If, in addition to this, a cold front comes and brings snow, more people could die. A large government can help us out, so it may not be such a bad idea after all."

That's what shifted the voters' minds slightly, leading to President Obama's victory by a small margin. It seems he received help from the divine.

However, the re-election of President Obama may lead to America's decline in the long run. This is the next issue.

His guardian spirit frequently mentioned 'One America'.

In this presidential election, the difference in number of electoral votes may have been over 100, but the difference in total share of votes across the country was very slim. It was nearly 50/50.

President Obama will need to greatly consider the opposing GOP votes.

As it is in Japan, the U.S. Congress remains divided with Democrats keeping the majority in the Senate

たくさん出た。さらに、寒波まで来て、雪が降り、凍え死ぬ人が出たりしたら、大変だ。大きな政府も、まんざら悪くはないのかな」と、多くの人々が思ったのです。

　そのため、有権者たちの考え方がかすかに振れて、オバマ大統領が僅差で勝ったのです。彼には、そういう天祐（天の助け）があったようですね。

　ただ、「オバマ大統領の再選は、大きな目で見ると、アメリカの衰退につながるのではないか」ということが、次なる疑問としてあるでしょう。

　彼の守護霊は、先ほど、「ワン・アメリカ（アメリカは一つ）」とよく言っていました。

　しかし、今回の大統領選では、獲得した「選挙人」の数では、両者の間に百人ぐらいの差がついたかもしれませんが、全米での両者の得票率自体を見ると、本当に僅差であり、ほぼ五分五分に近い戦いだったのです。

　したがって、オバマ大統領は、自分への反対票に対して、そうとう配慮しなくてはならないでしょう。

　また、アメリカの議会は、上院では民主党が多数、下院では共和党が多数であり、日本と同様に「ねじれ議会」

and Republicans keeping the majority in the House of Representatives. Therefore, President Obama will most likely take the policies closer to that of Republicans and more or less change his original policies.

Nevertheless, he will try to save the unemployed who he promised to save before. He wants to do his best regarding this. He will most likely attempt to create more jobs and employment.

## 11 A Secretary of State Other than Hillary May Accelerate Chinese Expansionism

Okawa　On a larger scale, we have another issue; it's whether the mission of America is to decline or not. The guardian spirit of President Obama said that it was none of his concern and that he had no clue as to what could possibly happen.

Since the U.S. is geographically a great distance away from China, they do not think of China as an enemy of war. Rather, they are hoping to make more

なので、今後、オバマ大統領は共和党寄りの政策をかなり採り、多少は従来の政策を変更すると思われます。

ただ、救済を約束していたのに救えなかった失業者たちを救おうとはするでしょう。これだけは、何としても、やりたいはずです。おそらく、職を増やそうと努力するだろうと思います。

## 11　ヒラリー氏以外の国務長官では、中国の増長を許す可能性がある

大川隆法　もう一段大きなマクロの問題、すなわち、「アメリカの使命が後退するかどうか」ということに関する、オバマ大統領の守護霊の見解は、「私の知ったことではない。私の予想の範囲を超えている」というものでした。

アメリカは、中国とは地理的にかなり距離があるので、中国を必ずしも戦争の相手とは考えていません。むしろ、「お互いに、まだ、もう少し稼げるのではないか」と思っ

## 1 Spiritual Interview with Re-elected President Obama

money in the mutual sense.

President Obama's guardian spirit is thinking, "The wealth amassed by both the U.S. and China can bring prosperity to the poor. This can be possible through good relations between the two countries."

On a different note, he remonstrated with us, saying Japan should refrain from provoking disputes with South Korea and China.

President Obama was re-elected but the Secretary of State Hillary Clinton is expected to resign from her position.

She was working on containing China, but what would happen if she resigns from her post? It would not matter as much if someone strong can take over her position. However, if a person not as strong or a so-called democratic person replaces her as the Secretary of State, I predict that he or she will take a tolerant approach against China. There is then a possibility of allowing China to expand even more.

We, Japan, can sense great danger since we are

第1章　再選したオバマ大統領のスピリチュアル・インタビュー

ています。

彼は、「その稼ぎによって、両国の貧しい人たちが潤うのではないか。両国がうまく付き合うことで、そのようにすることができるのではないか」と考えています。

一方、日本に対しては、「あまり韓国や中国と喧嘩をしてくれるな」と諫めるような感じでした。

オバマ大統領は再選されましたが、「ヒラリー・クリントン氏は国務長官を退くのではないか」と言われています。

彼女は「チャイナ包囲網」の構築に入っていたのですが、彼女が国務長官から外れた場合、どうなるでしょうか。後任が「強い人」であれば別ですが、それほど強くなく、いわゆる民主党的な人物が国務長官になるのであれば、私の予想では、中国に対して宥和政策に出ると思います。そのため、中国の増長を許す可能性があるのです。

日本は、地理的に中国と近いので、中国に対し、もの

geographically located near China. On the other hand, as I previously mentioned, the U.S. does not share our sense of crisis since they are a greater distance away.

Even if we tell them, "China might launch intercontinental missiles," they are probably thinking, "We'll do something about those missiles before they reach us." They still do not take China as a serious threat.

President Obama's guardian spirit said that the one who battles against China would probably be the next President – a Republican President, not him. It's an irresponsible statement, but most likely is his true thoughts. He seems to be thinking that there won't be a war with China during his next four-year term as President.

That may be true. There may not be a nuclear war between China and the U.S. in the next four years. It is less than likely.

In the meantime, though, China will gain more

第1章　再選したオバマ大統領のスピリチュアル・インタビュー

すごい危機を感じるのですが、先ほども述べたように、アメリカは、中国とは距離があるので、それほど危機を感じていません。

「中国が大陸間弾道弾を撃ってくるかもしれない」と言われても、「それが届くまでの間に、どうにかしますよ」と考えている程度でしょう。まだ中国を本気で脅威とは思っていないのです。

オバマ大統領の守護霊は、「中国と戦うのは、次の大統領、おそらくリパブリカン（共和党員）の大統領であって、自分ではないだろう」と言っていたので、無責任なところはありますが、それが本音でしょう。「私の次の任期の４年間には、中国との戦争はないだろう」と思っているようです。

確かに、中国とアメリカが核戦争をすることは、次の４年間ぐらいにはないでしょう。おそらく、ないと思います。

ただ、その間に、中国のほうは力をつけてきます。

1 Spiritual Interview with Re-elected President Obama

power.

A U.S.-China war may not happen in the next four years, but it may become unclear around the year 2020. He thinks this is all irrelevant to him because he won't be serving as President at that time. If he says so, then nothing can be done.

He probably hopes to educate the poor and the discriminated minorities in America, create new industries, create jobs and strengthen the economy one more time before his time is up.

He does seem to know the limits to the mission of America.

Geopolitical positioning has a lot to do with sensing threats from foreign countries. That is why America's attitude toward China is how it is.

Conversely, drug trafficking in Central and South America such as Cuba, Haiti and Nicaragua are of great concern in the U.S., but Japan does not sense any danger from that. That's how it is.

The feeling of distance between the U.S. and Central

第1章　再選したオバマ大統領のスピリチュアル・インタビュー

　次の４年間ぐらいでは、米中の戦争はないでしょうが、2020年ごろになると、「そろそろ分からない」という感じになるでしょう。でも、オバマ大統領にとっては、「そのとき、私は大統領をしていないから、関係ない」ということのようです。そう言われてしまえば、それまでです。

　彼は、「それまでに、アメリカの貧民層や、差別されているマイノリティーに教育をつけ、新しい産業をつくり、職を増やし、もう一回、経済を強くしておいたほうがよい」と思っているのでしょうか。

　「いちおう、アメリカの使命の限界を知ってはいる」と感じました。

　他国の脅威は、地政学的な位置関係によって感じられるものでもあるので、中国に対するアメリカの態度には、しかたがない面もあるでしょう。

　逆に、アメリカから見れば、キューバやハイチ、ニカラグア等、中南米の国による「麻薬の売り込み」などは、大変な問題なのですが、日本は、それに対して、何も脅威を感じません。そういうところがあるわけです。

　アメリカと中南米の距離感は、「日本」対「韓国や北朝

and South America is similar to that of between Japan and South Korea, North Korea or China.

The U.S. also thinks that Central and South America is the root of evil in their country.

Drug and human trafficking are conducted there. The mafia also comes to the U.S. from that region. That is why Central and South America seems to be the sink of iniquity.

Yet, the Japanese have little concern for them.

Geopolitics does play a role in this sense.

We, Happy Science, would like to pray that those who are pro-Japanese will serve in key positions in the U.S. government. At the same time, we must carry out our activities to seek understanding from President Obama and members of the new Cabinet.

I wonder what our Regional Director of the North America Headquarters is doing. (*laughs*) Is he actually working? He may be thinking, "Someone

第1章　再選したオバマ大統領のスピリチュアル・インタビュー

鮮、中国」の距離感と似ています。

　アメリカには、「要するに、中南米が、アメリカを悪くしている元凶だ」という考え方もあります。

　中南米では人身売買や麻薬の密輸入が行われていますし、中南米から、ヤクザまがいの人たち、マフィアが、たくさんアメリカに入ってくるので、アメリカには、中南米が悪の巣窟のように見えるのです。

　しかし、日本人には、中南米に対する関心は、あまりないわけです。

　そのようなところは、地政学的に、どうしてもあると感じられます。

　当会としては、アメリカにおいて、できるだけ知日派の人が要職に就いてくれることを祈りたいと思いますし、それと同時に、オバマ大統領や、次の政権で重要な閣僚になった方に対して、できるだけ日本への理解を求める運動をしなくてはいけないと思っています。

　当会のアメリカ本部長が、しっかりと仕事をしているのかどうか、よく知りません（笑）。あまり仕事をしていないのでしょうか。あちらも、「10年後の人がやるでしょ

in my position ten years later will do it" or "There is no need for me to do anything during Obama's presidency."

I said some time ago that I want to hold a lecture at the Yankee Stadium in America. People may think this is nonsense, but my objective is to also promote our teachings there so that we can have American people listen to what we have to say.

Thus, we should not let go of our dreams so easily.

It's impossible to move people if we do not have enough power of influence.

## 12  Japan Must Strengthen Their Self-Defense

**Okawa**  Today's interview made very clear as to what President Obama's thinking is.

Let's see how it turns out.

う」と言っているかもしれませんし、「オバマさんの任期中には、特に何かをする必要はない」と考えているかもしれません。

　私は、以前、「アメリカのヤンキースタジアムで講演をしたい」と述べたことがあります。世間の人たちは、「そんな無謀なことを考えるものではない」と思うのでしょうが、その狙いは、「そこでの講演によって、当会の教えのＰＲができれば、当会の言うことをアメリカの人々にも聴いてもらえるようになる」ということでもあるのです。

　そういう面もあるので、あっさりと夢を捨てないほうがよいと考えています。

　人々を動かそうとしても、やはり、こちらに、ある程度の勢力がないと、動かないものは動かないのです。

## 12　日本は自主防衛を強化したほうがよい

大川隆法　今日の収録で、オバマ大統領の考え方は、だいたい分かりました。

　あとは、今後どうなるか、見ていきましょう。

1 Spiritual Interview with Re-elected President Obama

I restrained myself, to some degree, from saying my predictions because they have a somewhat frightful side to it. But I said what I wanted to say.

I have said repeatedly throughout this whole year, "Protect our country on our own." I had foreseen that President Obama would be re-elected. It's just that I did not say it clearly. That's all.

We, Japan, must defend our country by ourselves in the next four years.

As evident in the interview, President Obama has no intention to fight against China. To him, the conflict over Senkaku is a small matter somewhere far, far away.

For example, just as we see internal struggles and conflicts over land issues between tribes in Africa as matters of a distant world seen from Japan, so is Senkaku issue seen from America.

It may have been a different story if President Obama lived not only in Indonesia but also in Japan

## 第1章 再選したオバマ大統領のスピリチュアル・インタビュー

　私の予言にも、少し怖い面があるので、今回は、そういう発言を控えめにしましたが、言いたいことは言いました。

　私は、今年、「自分の国は自分で守れ」と、一生懸命に訴えていましたが、それは、ある程度、「オバマ大統領が次の大統領選で勝つのではないか」と予想してのことでした。その予想を、はっきりとは言わなかっただけです。

　日本は、これからの４年間、自分の国を自分で守らなくてはいけません。

　今回の守護霊インタビューを聴いても、オバマ大統領には中国と戦う気がありません。彼にとっては、尖閣諸島をめぐる紛争など、遠い所における、とても小さな話にしかすぎないのです。

　例えば、アフリカで、部族同士が戦争をしたり、争ったり、土地の取り合いをしたりしていても、日本から見ると、遠い世界の出来事であり、どうでもいいことのように見えるでしょうが、アメリカには、尖閣諸島の問題が、そのように見えているところはあると思います。

　オバマ大統領が、過去、インドネシアだけではなく、日本にも何年か住んでくれていたら、話は少し違うのか

for several years in the past; but that's that. There is no complete human; there is always something missing.

If today's interview gets published as a book, then it may have some kind of influence.

We were able to interview the guardian spirit of President Obama immediately after his re-election. There are no Japanese media that can do this, so this interview will be a source of information for them. It will give a certain guideline to the Japanese government as well.

The Japanese government and the Foreign Ministry of Japan are probably relying on the U.S., but we clearly showed during this interview what exactly President Obama is thinking about. They are very adept at analyzing abstract words and meanings, so I'm sure they will understand what he meant.

In short, President Obama is saying that Japan must solve the issues over Takeshima and Senkaku islands on their own, without depending on America. To do so, Japan needs to be friends with South Korea and China.

## 第1章　再選したオバマ大統領のスピリチュアル・インタビュー

もしれませんが、まあ、いいでしょう。人間は、誰しも完全ではないので、足りないところはあるでしょう。

今日のインタビューが本になって出れば、何らかの影響はあるかもしれません。

再選早々、オバマ大統領（守護霊）へのインタビューができたわけですが、日本のメディアで、これができるところはないでしょうから、これは一つの情報源になるでしょうし、日本政府にとっても、一定の指針にはなると思います。

日本の政府や外務省は、おそらく、「アメリカ頼り」でいると思うのですが、今回、「オバマ大統領は、このように考えている」ということをお示ししました。抽象的な言語や遠回しな言葉の意味を読み取る能力が高い彼らには、「これは、どういうことか」が分かるでしょう。

要するに、オバマ大統領は、「竹島問題も尖閣問題も、アメリカに頼らず、日本で解決しなさい。そのためには、韓国や中国と友達になればよいのだ。仲良くしなさい。まあ、そういうことだ」と言っているのです。

Be friendly to each other. That's what he is saying.

When asked what America would ultimately do for Japan, his guardian spirit said that, in the end, President Obama would say that America will protect Japan. They may not provide the funds or military forces, but he would *say* America will protect Japan. That was the answer by his guardian spirit.

This is the sort of promise between U.S. and Japan.

Therefore, we must strengthen our self-defense in the next four years. That is my conclusion.

MC   Thank you very much, Master Ryuho Okawa.

第1章　再選したオバマ大統領のスピリチュアル・インタビュー

　そして、「アメリカは、最後には、日本に何をしてくれるのですか」という問いに対しては、「アメリカは、最後には、『日本を守る』ということぐらいは言うだろう。お金や軍隊は出さないかもしれないが、口では、『日本を守る』と言うかもしれない」と答えていました。

　このあたりが約束としてはあるわけです。
　したがって、このあとの４年間、日本は自主防衛を強化したほうがよいのです。これが私の結論です。

司会　大川隆法総裁、ありがとうございました。

# Chapter Two:
# Discourse with Obama

——An Interview with the Guardian Spirit of Obama——

> This spiritual message was recorded on the day after the previous U.S. presidential election (November 4, 2008). As this message contains valuable information and prophetic content, in time with president Obama's re-election, this message has been published as chapter two of this book. There are two questioners referred to as "A" and "B".

November 5, 2008, at Taigokan of Happy Science
Spiritual Messages from the Guardian Spirit of Barack Obama

# 第2章
# オバマとの対話
―― オバマ守護霊インタビュー ――

> 本霊言は、前回のアメリカ大統領選（2008年11月4日）の翌日に収録したものである。予言的内容をも含む、4年前の貴重な資料であるため、今回、オバマ大統領の再選に当たり、本書第2章として所収することとした。なお、質問者はA・Bと表記。

2008年11月5日 幸福の科学教祖殿 大悟館にて
バラク・オバマ守護霊の霊示

# 1 Summoning Mr. Obama's Guardian Spirit

A⸺ Mr. Obama, Mr. Obama, are you present? Recently elected U.S. president, Mr. Obama, are you there?

Obama's G.S.   Yes.

A⸺ Can you speak Japanese?

Obama's G.S.   No.

A⸺ Not even simple Japanese?

Obama's G.S.   It's difficult.

A⸺ Then we'll conduct this interview in English.

Obama's G.S.   Ah, OK.

# 1 オバマ氏の守護霊を招霊する

A―― オバマさん、オバマさん、いらっしゃいますか。今回、アメリカの大統領になったオバマさんはいらっしゃいますか。

オバマ守護霊　はい。

A―― 日本語は話せますか。

オバマ守護霊　いいえ。

A―― 片言の日本語も駄目ですか。

オバマ守護霊　難しい。

A―― では、英語でやってみましょう。

オバマ守護霊　ああ、オーケー。

2 Discourse with Obama

A⸻ Who were you in your past life?

Obama's G.S.  What's that?

B⸻ Who were you before you were born?

Obama's G.S.  What do you mean?

B⸻ Have you ever been born in another country before?

Obama's G.S.  Oh, I don't know. I don't know. What do you mean? I don't understand what you want to say. I don't understand.

B⸻ Do you know about the other world?

Obama's G.S.  What do you mean by the other world?

第2章　オバマとの対話

A——　あなたの過去世(かこぜ)は誰(だれ)ですか。

**オバマ守護霊**　それは何ですか。

B——　あなたは、今回、生まれる前の人生では誰でしたか。

**オバマ守護霊**　どういう意味ですか。

B——　あなたには、以前、他の国に生まれたことがありませんか。

**オバマ守護霊**　ああ、分かりません。分かりません。どういう意味ですか。何が言いたいのかが分かりません。私には理解できません。

B——　あの世はご存じですか。

**オバマ守護霊**　あの世とは何のことですか。

2 Discourse with Obama

B——  Do you know where people go to after death?

**Obama's G.S.**  Ah-hah. You mean Heaven or Hell? I got it. I understand.

B——  Have you been born before you were born as Obama?

**Obama's G.S.**  Uh-huh. In Christianity, it's forbidden to believe in reincarnation, so I myself don't believe in reincarnation. I know there is some spiritual being indeed, but I cannot explain it correctly. So we have a very different way of thinking.

B——  I understand. Do you believe that you have been born before? Do you believe in reincarnation?

**Obama's G.S.**  I'm not sure. But I'm the guardian spirit of Obama. It's true. I know. But I can't say

第2章　オバマとの対話

B――　死後、人はどこへ行くか、分かりますか。

**オバマ守護霊**　ああ。天国・地獄(じごく)という意味ですか。分かりました。理解できます。

B――　あなたは、今回オバマとして生まれる前に、生まれたことがありますか。

**オバマ守護霊**　ああ。キリスト教では転生輪廻(てんしょうりんね)を信じることは禁じられているので、私自身は転生輪廻を信じていません。何らかの霊的(れいてき)存在がいるのは分かりますが、私には正確に説明できません。あなたたちと私の考え方は大きく異なります。

B――　分かりました。あなた自身としては、かつて生まれたことがあると信じますか。転生輪廻は？

**オバマ守護霊**　よく分かりません。しかし、私がオバマの守護霊であることは確かです。それは分かります。し

## 2 Discourse with Obama

whether or not this means I have reincarnated. I am the guardian spirit of Barack Obama, but I don't know what that means.

B—— You can't remember…?

Obama's G.S.   You mean about me? Or Obama?

B—— About yourself.

Obama's G.S.   I'm an angel.

B—— May I ask your name?

Obama's G.S.   My name? Uh-huh. Hmm… my name… This is the first time for me. My first experience. Who are you?

B—— My name is ○○.

かし、それが転生輪廻を意味するかは分かりません。私はバラク・オバマの守護霊ですが、その意味するところは分かりません。

B―― 思い出せませんか。

オバマ守護霊　私のこと？　それともオバマのこと？

B―― あなたのことです。

オバマ守護霊　私は天使です。

B―― あなたの名前を伺ってもよろしいですか。

オバマ守護霊　私の名前？　ああ、うーん、私の名前……、これは私にとって初めてのことであり、初めての経験ですね。あなたは誰ですか。

B―― 私は○○といいます。

2 Discourse with Obama

**Obama's G.S.**  Who are you?

B——  I want to know about Mr. Obama's past and Mr. Obama's thoughts about this world and America.

**Obama's G.S.**  Yeah, I can explain about that, but I can't explain reincarnation correctly. In Christianity it's forbidden, so I cannot talk about it. But I can tell you about his thoughts and opinions.

B——  OK.

## 2 He Has No Idea on How to Solve America's Financial Problems

B——  So, my first question is, what do you think about America's financial problems?

**Obama's G.S.**  It's very difficult. We need patience.

オバマ守護霊　あなたは誰ですか。

B──　私は、オバマ氏の過去と、アメリカと世界についてのオバマ氏の考えを知りたいのです。

オバマ守護霊　それなら説明できますが、転生輪廻については正確に説明することはできません。キリスト教では禁じられているので、言えないのです。しかし、彼の考えや意見について述べることはできます。

B──　分かりました。

## 2　金融危機を救うアイデアはない

B──　では、最初の質問ですが、アメリカの金融問題（リーマン・ショック）について、どう考えておられますか。

オバマ守護霊　非常に難しいです。われわれには忍耐が

We need more than four years to conquer this economic crisis. I want to collect taxes from the rich people and I want to give this money to the poor.

But exactly speaking, I'm not sure how to deal with this matter, so I must think about it by next January (2009, when he takes office). I must make up my mind on this matter, but it's very difficult.

No one can conquer this economic crisis, this financial crisis. It's the first time for the people living today, so it's very difficult.

But I have been talking about change, so I will change us. I must change America. I hope that there will be some kind of new wave or new wind that will assist us. The mood of this country will change and I will ask our people to do their best. I am younger than McCain so I can understand this difficult matter, and I can fight against this difficult matter.

I'll do my best. I must make a new law regarding economics. This is my next step so I can't say anymore at this time, but this is very difficult. No one

必要です。この経済危機を克服するには４年以上は必要でしょう。私は、お金持ちから税金を取って、貧しい人たちに与えたいと思います。

しかし、正確に言うと、この事態をどう対処すべきかは分からないので、（大統領に就任する）来年（2009年）１月までに考えなければいけません。この問題について考えをまとめなければなりませんが、非常に難しいのです。

この経済危機、金融危機を克服できる人は誰もいません。今、生きている人間にとって初めてのことなので、本当に難しいのです。

しかし、私は「チェインジ」を訴えてきたので、変えてみせます。アメリカを変えなければならないのです。何らかの新しい波、新しい風が来て、われわれを助けてくれることを願っています。そして、アメリカの空気が変わるでしょう。国民には頑張ってくれることを求めます。私は、マケインより若いので、この難しい事態を理解できますし、この問題と戦うことができます。

ベストを尽くします。私は、経済に関する新しい法律をつくらなければなりません。それは次のステップなので、現時点では、これ以上は言えませんが、非常に難し

can solve this problem. I must endure for four years at least. It's extremely difficult.

To tell the truth, I have no idea (what I'm doing). I am just saying, "Change," and "Change" only. I don't have a radical idea.

# 3 My Main Concern is America's Domestic Issues

B—— Then next, may I ask you about Japan? What do you think about Japan?

Obama's G.S.　Hmm… hmm… That's not an easy question. OK, I understand you are Japanese people…

B—— Do you think that you should cooperate with Japan or should Japan be independent?

い問題であることは確かです。この問題を解決できる人はいません。少なくとも４年間は耐えなければいけません。たいへん難しいのです。

　正直に言うと、さっぱり分からないので、ただ、「チェインジ」を訴えているわけです。とにかく、「チェインジ」あるのみです。抜本的なアイデアがあるわけではありません。

## 3　主な関心は「アメリカ国内」にある

Ｂ──　次に、日本についてお訊きしてもよろしいでしょうか。日本については、どうお考えでしょうか。

**オバマ守護霊**　うーん、うーん。これはそんなに易しい質問ではないですね。オーケー。あなたがたが日本人であることは理解していますが……。

Ｂ──　あなたは、「日本と協力すべき」とお考えですか。それとも、「日本は自立すべき」とお考えですか。

**Obama's G.S.**  Yeah, we must cooperate with each other, but the direction will be a little different from now on. We are not Republican, so my main concern is about America itself, the United States, and the equality of the people, especially black people.

I must concentrate on realizing this equality. Equality is the starting point of democracy. So I must concentrate on saving the poor people in America who are not given enough chances. So this is my best plan. Japan is secondary, I think. Japan is so far east…

## 4  I Want to Speak with the Great China Rather than Japan

B——  Next, may I ask about China? What do you think about China?

**Obama's G.S.**  It's a great country. It is a gigantic

**オバマ守護霊** そうですね、われわれは協力しなければいけませんが、今後は方向性が少し違ってきます。私たちは共和党ではないので、私の主な関心は、アメリカ自体、つまり合衆国のことにあり、国民の平等、特に黒人の平等にあるのです。

　私は、この平等のために全力を注がなければなりません。平等は民主主義の出発点です。私は、「アメリカにいる、十分なチャンスを与えられていない貧しい人々をどのように救うか」ということに、全力を挙げなければなりません。これが私の最善の計画です。日本は二の次と考えています。極東ですから……。

## 4　日本よりも「偉大な中国」と話がしたい

Ｂ――　次に、中国についてお訊きしてもよろしいでしょうか。中国については、どうお考えですか。

**オバマ守護霊**　中国は偉大な国です。長い長い歴史を持

nation with a long, long history, so we must be friends with Chinese people. We must be close friends with China, so I want to make a hot line with China's top leader, talk with him and decide the direction of the world. This is very easy and could instantly solve world problems, so I'm aiming to be a good friend of China's top leader. I think it's a great country.

My understanding is that Japan is like Hawaii or California from China's perspective, so I want to talk to the Chinese leaders first.

Japanese people cannot decide their own opinions, even their own opinions. They need time to decide something and I don't know who I should talk with or who makes the decisions in Japan, so I want to talk with China first.

つ、巨大な国です。ですから、われわれは、中国の人々と友好的でなくてはなりません。われわれは中国と緊密な友好関係を結ぶべきです。私は、中国の首脳とホットラインを結び、話し合い、世界の方向性をつくり上げていきたいと考えています。これは、世界の問題を解決するための、非常に簡単かつ直ちに実行できる方法です。私は、中国首脳とよき友人になることを目指しています。中国は偉大な国だと思います。

　私の見解では、日本は、中国から見ると、ハワイかカリフォルニアのようなものなので、私は、まず中国の首脳と話がしたいのです。


　日本人は、自分自身の意見を決めることができません。自分自身の意見さえもです。彼らは、何を決めるにしても時間がかかります。「誰と話をすべきか」「誰が日本の決断を行うのか」が私には分からないのです。ですから、私はまず中国と話がしたいのです。

# 5 I am Not Interested in Korea and Taiwan

B—— Next, may I ask about Korea? South Korea and North Korea.

**Obama's G.S.** That is Korea's matter. They should talk with each other and they should decide for themselves. The top leaders, of North and South Korea, and the people should discuss this matter. They should discuss this matter, this long-lasting problem.

It's up to them whether or not North and South Korea should be one country, or whether they choose to be friends with China or Japan. It depends on them, so I am not concerned about that.

B—— May I ask about Taiwan?

**Obama's G.S.** Taiwan is a small island. I can't use the U.S. forces for the matter between Taiwan and

## 5 朝鮮と台湾については関心がない

B ── 次に、朝鮮についてお訊きしてもよろしいでしょうか。韓国と北朝鮮です。

**オバマ守護霊** それは朝鮮の人々の問題だと思います。彼らが互いに話し合い、彼ら自身で決めるべきです。北朝鮮および韓国の首脳と国民が、この問題について議論すべきです。長期にわたるこれらの問題については、彼らが議論すべきなのです。
　南北朝鮮を統一するかしないかは、彼らの決断次第です。また、彼らが中国あるいは日本と友好関係を結ぶかどうかも、彼ら次第です。私は、そのことにはまったく関心がありません。

B ── 台湾については、いかがですか。

**オバマ守護霊** 台湾は小さな島です。私は、中台問題のためにアメリカの軍事力を使うことはできません。われ

China. We must stay neutral; we will just observe them. They should talk with each other. It's their own matter. So whether Taiwan is a part of China or not is not an American matter. It's their matter.

B—— So whether Taiwan and China are close or not is their own matter and America does not care?

**Obama's G.S.** Yeah. I don't want to use any military forces for this matter.

# 6 America Will No Longer be The World Policeman

B—— I want to ask for your basic thoughts on Muslims and terrorism.

**Obama's G.S.** I think the Iraqi War was wrong. It was a wrong decision made by the Republican

われは中立でなければなりません。われわれは、ただ見ているだけです。彼らは、お互いに話し合うべきです。これは彼らの問題です。台湾が中国の一部であるかどうかは、アメリカの問題ではありません。彼らの問題です。

B──　つまり、「台湾と中国が接近するかどうかは彼らの問題であり、アメリカは関与しない」ということでしょうか。

オバマ守護霊　そうです。私は、この問題のためにアメリカの軍隊を使いたくはありません。

## 6　将来、アメリカは「世界の警察」ではなくなる

B──　では、次に、イスラム教徒とテロに関しての、あなたの基本的な考えをお訊きしたいと思います。

オバマ守護霊　私はイラク戦争を間違いだったと考えています。共和党の大統領が間違った判断を下したのです。

president. It was a bad thing. They are just intruders so I want to have the army retreat, and I want to save the military budget. I want to cut costs and reduce the financial deficit. Most of our financial loss is due to the military budget.

So I don't want to start any wars from now on, and there will be peace, *Obama Peace*, in the world, on this Earth. During my presidency, there shall be no wars on Earth. People want a peaceful period. I think so and I hope so.

B—— What will you do to prevent terrorism?

**Obama's G.S.** I will just talk with them. Islam is not a bad religion. I will just talk to them and ask them to stop their terrorist attacks. Also, the United States of America will not attack them from now on. So we must make peace on earth. During my presidency, I will aim to create an age of peace, an age without

Note p.190

これは悪いことです。彼らは、ただの侵略者ですから、私はこの軍隊を撤退させたいと思っています。そして、軍事予算を縮小したいと考えています。コストカットして、アメリカの財政赤字を削減したいのです。財政赤字は、ほとんど軍事予算によって発生しているわけですからね。

　私は、今後いかなる戦争も起こさないつもりです。その結果、"オバマの平和"が、世界に、この地球上に訪れるでしょう。私の大統領就任期間中は、地球上から戦争がなくなるはずです。人々は平和の時代が来ることを望んでいると思いますし、私もそれを望んでいます。


B──　テロをどのように防ぐおつもりですか。


**オバマ守護霊**　とにかく話し合うことです。彼らと対話することです。イスラム教は悪い宗教ではありません。私は、彼らと話し合って、テロをやめるように要望します。アメリカ合衆国もまた、今後、彼らを攻撃することはないでしょう。私たちは地上に平和をつくり上げなければなりません。私の就任期間中は、平和でテロのない

terrorism.

B—— Do you think the United States should play the role of the world policeman?

**Obama's G.S.**  No, that is a bad way of thinking. America should concentrate on their own issues. America has a lot of problems, so we must settle these problems. America will not act as the world policeman in the future. Every country should defend themselves on their own. America will not attack any countries, I promise.

> Note: After taking office as president, Obama began a large-scale sweeping operation against the Taliban in Afghanistan. In 2011, the US forces killed the al-Qaeda leader Osama bin Laden in a military operation ordered by Obama.

第2章　オバマとの対話

時代を目指します。

B──　あなたは、アメリカ合衆国が「世界の警察」の役割を果たすべきとお考えでしょうか。

**オバマ守護霊**　いや、それはよくない考え方です。アメリカは、自分たちの問題に集中すべきです。アメリカは、国内に多くの問題を抱(かか)えていて、これらの多くの問題を解決しなければなりません。ですから、将来、アメリカは「世界の警察」ではなくなるのです。どの国も自国防衛を考えるべきです。アメリカは、今後、どの国も攻撃しないことを約束します。


〔注〕ただし、オバマ氏は大統領就任後、アフガニスタンで、大規模なタリバン掃討作戦を開始。2011年には、軍事作戦によってアルカイダの指導者ウサマ・ビン・ラディンを殺害している。

# 7  Are Rich People Evil Existences?

B —— I want to ask about your thoughts on wealth and rich people. What do you think about them?

**Obama's G.S.**  I don't like them. They are too arrogant and they are evil toward poor people, especially immigrants. So, I don't like them.

A —— Do you have an inferiority complex?

**Obama's G.S.**  No. No. It's justice. I'm seeking for justice.

B —— You don't think that the rich people made the United States or that they make United States stable?

**Obama's G.S.**  1% of the rich people of the United States has 90% of America's wealth. I think it's a bad thing. It's not good.

# 7 富裕層は「邪悪な存在」？

B── では、富や富裕層に対するあなたの考えをお訊きしたいと思います。彼らについて、どうお考えですか。

オバマ守護霊　彼らは好きではありません。彼らは傲慢すぎます。貧しい人々、特に移民にとっては邪悪な存在です。ですから、好きではありません。

A── それは劣等感ですか。

オバマ守護霊　違う、違う。正義ですよ。私は正義を追求しているのです。

B── あなたは、豊かな人々がアメリカを成り立たせ、安定させているとは思わないのですか。

オバマ守護霊　わずか1パーセントのお金持ちが、アメリカの資産の90パーセントを持っています。これは悪いことです。よくないと思います。

So I want to change this country, and I also want to save, of course, African people, Asian people and poor people. I think it's the Will of God.

## 8  His True Feelings: The Japanese are Sneaky People

B—— So, do you think Japan should cooperate with the world? Or should the Japanese concentrate only on their country?

**Obama's G.S.**  Hmm… Japan… they already have enough; they are happy. They live happily enough, so they should be required not to seek for more wealth. It's enough.

They're already rich because of our assistance, so the United States should assist other poor countries. Japan should stand up on their own feet. The poor countries need more assistance.

If Japan has a problem regarding Self-Defense

ですから、私は、この国を変え、アフリカ系やアジア系の人々、貧しい人々を救いたいのです。これは神の意志だと思います。

## 8 「日本はアメリカの敵」という本音

B──　では、「日本は、世界に貢献（こうけん）すべきとお考えですか、それとも世界に貢献するのではなく、日本のことだけに集中すればよい」とお考えですか。

**オバマ守護霊**　うーん、日本……。彼らはもう十分です。彼らは幸福です。十分、幸福に暮らしているのだから、これ以上、豊かになろうとするのはやめるべきでしょう。もう十分です。

　日本は、アメリカに助けてもらって、すでにお金持ちになっているので、アメリカは、ほかの貧しい国を助けるべきです。日本は、自分の足で立つべきでしょう。貧しい国は、助けを必要としています。

　日本が自衛隊について問題を抱（かか）えているのなら、自分

Force, they should change it by themselves. America has no concern about that. No advice. They should make up their mind. They must be strong. They are strong enough now. It's time. It's up to Japan. It's up to the Japanese people as to whether they become stronger or weaker. They should make up their mind.

The Japanese leader, the prime minister, should make up that policy, but I feel that Japanese leaders have never decided on any crucial problems. So they are not a country. I must choose my word carefully, but can you understand the word *irritated*? I have that kind of feeling.

They don't speak straightforwardly, so it takes a long time to talk with Japanese people. They have no conclusion. They just sit around for procedure and there is no conclusion. It's an old-styled, old-fashioned style of politics. I hate this kind of style.

B—— So, do you think that U.S.-Japan Security Treaty is not that important?

たちの手で変革すべきです。アメリカはそれに関心がありません。アドバイスもしません。自分たちで決めるべきです。日本は強くならなければいけません。もう十分に強いはずです。今がそのときです。日本次第(しだい)ですよ。日本がより強くなるのか、それとも弱くなるのかは、日本人次第でしょう。自分たちで決めるべきです。

　日本の指導者である首相が政策を決めるべきですが、彼らは、いつも、重大な問題についての決断を避(さ)けてきたように感じます。これでは国家とは言えません。彼らは……、言葉を選ばないといけませんが、「イライラする」という言葉は分かりますか。私はそう感じます。


　彼らははっきり言わないので、日本人と話すのには手間がかかります。彼らには結論がありません。プロセスばかりに費(つい)やして、結論がないのです。これは古いスタイルです。時代遅(おく)れの政治スタイルです。私はそういうやり方が大嫌(だいきら)いです。

B──　ということは、「日米安全保障条約は重要ではない」ということでしょうか。

## 2 Discourse with Obama

**Obama's G.S.**　It's not so important. It's time to reconsider the U.S. and Japanese military treaty. We don't need such kind of special relationship anymore. Japan is one of the Asian countries and an economic giant, so they can be independent. They need no more assistance from us.

In some meaning, they are our enemies. We are competitors, but in the near future, American people will have more hope toward China. There are a lot of people in China and they will buy American goods, so America can overcome this economic recession.

But Japanese people, even when the Yen is strong, don't buy American goods. They are evil people. They are thinking only about their own profit. We are not equal partners.

B──　So you don't think that United States and Japan are equal partners?

**オバマ守護霊** それほど重要ではありません。日米の軍事協定は見直す時期に来ています。もう、そういう特別な関係は必要ありません。日本はアジアの一国であり、経済大国ですから、自立できるでしょう。われわれの助けは必要ありません。

　日本は、ある意味で、われわれの敵です。日本とアメリカは競合者なのです。それに、近い将来においては、中国のほうに、アメリカ人は期待を寄せるでしょう。中国は、人口が多く、アメリカの商品を買ってくれるでしょう。それで、アメリカは不況を脱出することができるのです。

　しかし、日本人は、円高になっても、アメリカの商品を買ってくれません。彼らは悪い人々です。自分の利益しか考えていません。対等な協力関係ではないのです。


Ｂ── 「日本とアメリカ合衆国は、対等な協力関係にはない」とお考えでしょうか。

**Obama's G.S.** Yeah, I think Japanese people are sneaky people. They did a sneak attack on Hawaii. I hate that. They are sneaky people. They have an evil tendency so they cannot be our equal partners. I think Japan is one of the strong Asian countries.

## 9 Is China the Future of America?

**Obama's G.S.** I will choose China. We have hopes for China. China is the future of America. We have a market in China, so I think it's the future of America. I will abandon Taiwan, and Japan next. I will choose China.

B—— That's simple.

**Obama's G.S.** It's simple, but smart.

A—— China is expanding their military power, and

オバマ守護霊 そう。日本人は卑怯な国民だと思います。ハワイも奇襲攻撃しました。嫌いですね。卑怯な国民です。性格が邪悪なので、対等の協力相手にはなりえないのです。単なるアジアの強国の一つだと思っています。

## 9 「中国はアメリカの未来」なのか

オバマ守護霊 私は中国を選びます。中国には希望があります。中国はアメリカの未来です。中国には市場があるから、アメリカの未来なのです。私は、まず台湾を捨て、次に日本を捨て、そして、中国を選びます。

B―― 単純ですね。

オバマ守護霊 単純ですが、賢明です。

A―― 中国は軍事拡張をしています。そして、核兵器の

there is also the issue of nuclear weapons…

Obama's G.S.  It's OK.

A——  OK!?

Obama's G.S.  They are a gigantic country. They have military enemies, so they need military forces, of course. There are a lot of bad countries around them; Russian forces, Japanese forces, and other countries such as India. They are surrounded by strong countries, so they should defend themselves.

It's OK as long as they don't attack America. We need a treaty between China and America. I think a military treaty is essential.

B——  You don't think that Korea is in a bad situation?

Obama's G.S.  Korea is a small country, so it's up to

問題も……。

**オバマ守護霊** それは構いません。

A―― 構わない⁉

**オバマ守護霊** 中国は巨大(きょだい)な国です。彼らには、軍事的に敵対する国がありますから、もちろん、軍事力が必要です。周辺には悪い国がたくさんあります。ロシア軍や日本軍やほかの国があります。インドもそうです。強国に囲まれているわけだから、防衛が必要なのです。

アメリカを攻(せ)めなければ構いません。米中の同盟が必要です。軍事同盟が必須(ひっす)となるでしょう。

B―― 朝鮮(ちょうせん)は険悪な状態にあると思いませんか。

**オバマ守護霊** 朝鮮は小さな国です。ですから、中国次(し)

China. China should give directions to Korea and its people.

B—— North Korea is starting to develop their military strength.

**Obama's G.S.** It's a small country. We can disregard them. They cannot attack America.

B—— So even if North Korea attacks Japan, is it only a problem between Japan and North Korea?

**Obama's G.S.** Yeah, it's their problem. Japan should retaliate. They have the Self-Defense Force so they can do that. Whether Japan retaliates or not is up to Japan or Japanese people. It's not the responsibility of the United States. It's Japan's problem.

B—— If Japan needs help, will the U.S. military help us?

第です。中国が、朝鮮と朝鮮の人々の方向を決めるべきでしょう。

B——　北朝鮮は軍事力を伸ばしています。

オバマ守護霊　小さな国です。無視できる大きさです。彼らはアメリカを攻撃できません。

B——　北朝鮮が日本を攻撃しても、それは、「日本と北朝鮮の問題」ということでしょうか。

オバマ守護霊　ああ、彼らの問題です。日本が、何らかの報復をすべきです。自衛隊があるのだから、自分たちでできるでしょう。報復するかどうかは、日本あるいは日本人の問題です。アメリカ合衆国には何の責任もありません。日本の問題です。

B——　日本が米軍に助けを求めたら、助けてくれるのでしょうか。

**Obama's G.S.**   No. We need China, so we would ask China to persuade North Korea. That's all.

A⎯⎯   Don't you think that America will be isolated?

**Obama's G.S.**   It's OK. Yeah, we are isolated now because of the difficult financial problem. We must solve this financial problem. I need at least four years to solve this matter, so I have no diplomatic desire for America to be the world policeman. I have no concern about that. America should not be the policeman of the world.

B⎯⎯   Is it OK to be isolated?

**Obama's G.S.**   Uh-huh. Yeah.

B⎯⎯   Don't you think that Japan is the only country

**オバマ守護霊** いや、助けません。私たちには中国が必要なので、中国に北朝鮮を説得するよう頼みます。それだけです。

A―― アメリカは孤立すると思いませんか。

**オバマ守護霊** 構いません。金融問題で手いっぱいであり、実際に孤立しています。私たちは、この問題を解決しなければなりません。少なくとも４年はかかります。ですから、私には、「アメリカが『世界の警察』になる」という、外交的な野心はないし、関心もありません。アメリカは、「世界の警察」になるべきではありません。

B―― 孤立してもよいのですか。

**オバマ守護霊** ええ、いいです。

B―― 「日本がアメリカの金融危機を救える唯一の国で

that can save America from their financial crisis?

**Obama's G.S.**  No, no, no, there are European countries and China. Japan is one option.

B⸺  One option?

**Obama's G.S.**  Yeah.

# 10  He Wants to Become a President More Famous than Lincoln

B⸺  You are the first U.S. president who is a black person. What do you think about that?

**Obama's G.S.**  I'm proud of that, of course. My name shall be engraved in the history of the United States. I want to be a black Kennedy or Lincoln. I want to be a very famous president.

This is the second founding of this nation. I'm the

ある」とは考えませんか。

オバマ守護霊　いや、いや、いや。ヨーロッパの国々もあれば、中国もあります。日本は一つの選択肢ですよ。

B──　一つの選択肢ですか。

オバマ守護霊　そうです。

## 10　リンカン以上の有名な大統領になりたい

B──　あなたは、合衆国で初めての黒人大統領ですが、そのことについて、どうお考えですか。

オバマ守護霊　もちろん誇りに思います。私の名前は合衆国の歴史に刻まれることになるでしょう。「黒人のケネディ」「黒人のリンカン」と言われるような、有名な大統領になりたいと思っています。
　これは第二の建国です。私は、第二のジョージ・ワシ

2 Discourse with Obama

second George Washington. Black people will have more power from now on, so it's the second creation of the nation. There is great hope for this country. Our future is promised.

B—— You don't need white people?

Obama's G.S.   Of course, I need white people, but they earn too much. They made enough money, so it's time to change America.

The minority should have power in the American government, our diplomacy, economy and financial world. It's the age of minorities.

B—— The age of minorities.

Obama's G.S.   Yeah.

B—— So you are very proud of being a minority?

ントンです。これからは、黒人が力を持つようになります。第二の建国です。この国には希望が満ち溢れています。私たちの未来は約束されているのです。

B── 白人は必要ないのでしょうか。

**オバマ守護霊** もちろん必要ですが、彼らは儲けすぎました。もう十分に儲けたのですから、今はアメリカを変革するときです。

　マイノリティー（少数派）の人々が、政府・外交・経済・金融において力を持つべきときです。マイノリティーの時代が来たのです。

B── マイノリティーの時代ですか。

**オバマ守護霊** そうです。

B── では、あなたは、自分がマイノリティーであることをたいへん誇りに思っているのでしょうか。

**Obama's G.S.**  Uh-huh. But I'm afraid I shall be assassinated in the near future. I'm afraid of that. White people will try to get revenge from me. I'm afraid of that. There is an 80% possibility. There is an 80% chance that it will happen in these four years. So, at that time, I can become an angel in Heaven, so it's OK.

Even Kennedy, Lincoln and Martin Luther King were assassinated, so I want to be assassinated as well. Then at that time, my name will be written on a golden plate, yeah, in the memory of the people forever. I want to be such kind of famous American president. I want to be more famous than Lincoln.

B—— What do you think is the most important thing for black people to become rich?

**Obama's G.S.**  Education is first. They need more opportunities to get an education. Next is promotion. They need equal promotion. Then next is wealth. At

第2章　オバマとの対話

**オバマ守護霊**　そうです。ただ、近い将来、暗殺されるのではないかと心配です。怖いですね。白人が何らかの報復に出るのではないかと思います。80パーセントの可能性があります。4年間に起きる可能性は80パーセントだと思います。まあ、そのときは、そのときで、私は天国で天使になれるだろうから、構いません。

　ケネディも、リンカンも、マーティン・ルーサー・キング牧師も暗殺されましたが、私もそうなりたいのです。そうすれば、私の名前は金板に刻まれ、そう、人々の記憶に永遠に遺ることができます。そういう有名なアメリカ大統領になりたいのです。私はリンカン以上になりたいのです。

B──　黒人が豊かになるために最も大切なことは、何だと思いますか。

**オバマ守護霊**　「教育」が第一です。もっと教育のチャンスが必要です。次は「社会的地位の向上」です。平等な地位向上の機会が必要です。その次に「富」です。少なくとも、

least 20 to 30% of America's wealth should be given to black people. That much wealth is produced by black people so they should receive the results. I hope so.

# 11  You Must Govern Your Nation by Yourself

B—— You have mentioned a lot about China. I want to ask you about BRICs.

**Obama's G.S.**  BRICs?

B—— Brazil, Russia, India…. Do you think they are important?

**Obama's G.S.**  Yeah, they are equal to Japan in my mind.

B—— Oh OK, so they should live on their own…

富の20～30パーセントは、黒人に与えられるべきです。それが黒人によって生み出されている以上、彼らは、その成果を受け取るべきです。そうなることを願っています。

## 11　自分たちの力で自国を治めるのが原則だ

B——　中国について、たくさん話をしていただきましたが、ブリックスについてはどうでしょうか。

**オバマ守護霊**　ブリックス？

B——　ブラジル、ロシア、インド……。これらの国々は重要だと思いますか。

**オバマ守護霊**　そうですね、私のなかでは、位置づけは日本と同じようなものです。

B——　ああ、では、「自分たちでやっていくべきだ」と……。

**Obama's G.S.**   Yeah. If we can expect any financial or diplomatic profit, I will cooperate with them. But, the principle is that all nations should make their own rules by themselves.

## 12   It's Time for Revenge

A——   Lastly, is there anything you would like to say to the people of the world?

**Obama's G.S.**   I'm the first black president, so I will change the world. The fact that I'm the first black president itself is a message from God. Historically, black people have suffered because of white people. We were attacked and ill-treated by white people.

It's time for revenge, yeah. "Black power" has been unleashed.

A——   OK, thank you very much.

オバマ守護霊 そうです。何か、金融面や外交面での利益がアメリカにあるのであれば、協力しますよ。しかし、原則としては、すべての国は、自分たちの力で自国を治めるべきでしょう。

## 12 今こそ、リベンジのとき

A── 最後に、世界の人たちに向けて、何か語りたいことはあるでしょうか。

オバマ守護霊 私は、初の黒人大統領ですから、世界を変えます。私が初の黒人大統領になったこと自体、神からのメッセージなのです。歴史的に、黒人は白人から苦しめられてきました。攻撃されたり、白人からひどい扱いを受けたりしてきました。
　今こそリベンジ（復讐）のときです。そう、黒人のパワーが解き放たれたのです。

A── 分かりました。ありがとうございました。

**Obama's G.S.**   Is it OK?

A—   OK.

**Obama's G.S.**   Oh you are good people. You speak good English, yeah. Bye.

A—   Bye-bye.

**オバマ守護霊** いいですか。

A—— はい。

**オバマ守護霊** あなたたちは、いい人です。英語も上手ですね。それでは。

A—— さようなら。

## *Afterword*

Have you understood the meaning of *Guardian Spirit*? Perhaps you are to be required a little more knowledge regarding *Buddha's Truth*.

We are the worldwide network of God.

We are working under the name of *Happy Science*. It's Japan's most huge and famous religious group. We also have a religious party, *the Happiness Realization Party*. That is the reason we have much concern about world politics and economics.

This book is expected to be read in both the United States and Japan. Also the readers of this book are scheduled to join the movement of creating worldwide Happiness. I hope so.

November 13, 2012
Master & CEO of Happy Science
Ryuho Okawa

## あとがき

　あなたは、守護霊の意味が理解できただろうか。おそらく、「仏法真理」に関して、もう少し知識が必要なはずだ。

　私たちは、神の世界的ネットワークである。

　私たちは、「幸福の科学」の名の下に活動している。幸福の科学は、日本で最も大きく有名な宗教団体である。私たちは、「幸福実現党」という宗教政党も持っている。したがって、私たちは、国際政治や経済についても非常に関心を持っている。

　本書は、アメリカ合衆国と日本の両方で読まれるだろう。そして、読者たちは、世界中の幸福創造の運動に参画していくことになるだろう。私はそう願っている。

2012 年 11 月 13 日
人類の教師・幸福の科学総裁
大川隆法

バラク・オバマのスピリチュアル・メッセージ
——再選大統領は世界に平和をもたらすか——

2012年11月27日　初版第1刷

著　者　　大川　隆法

発　行　　幸福実現党
〒107-0052　東京都港区赤坂2丁目10番8号
TEL(03)6441-0754

発　売　　幸福の科学出版株式会社
〒107-0052　東京都港区赤坂2丁目10番14号
TEL(03)5573-7700
http://www.irhpress.co.jp/

印刷・製本　株式会社 堀内印刷所

落丁・乱丁本はおとりかえいたします
©Ryuho Okawa 2012. Printed in Japan. 検印省略
ISBN978-4-86395-271-3 C0030
Photo: ロイター/アフロ

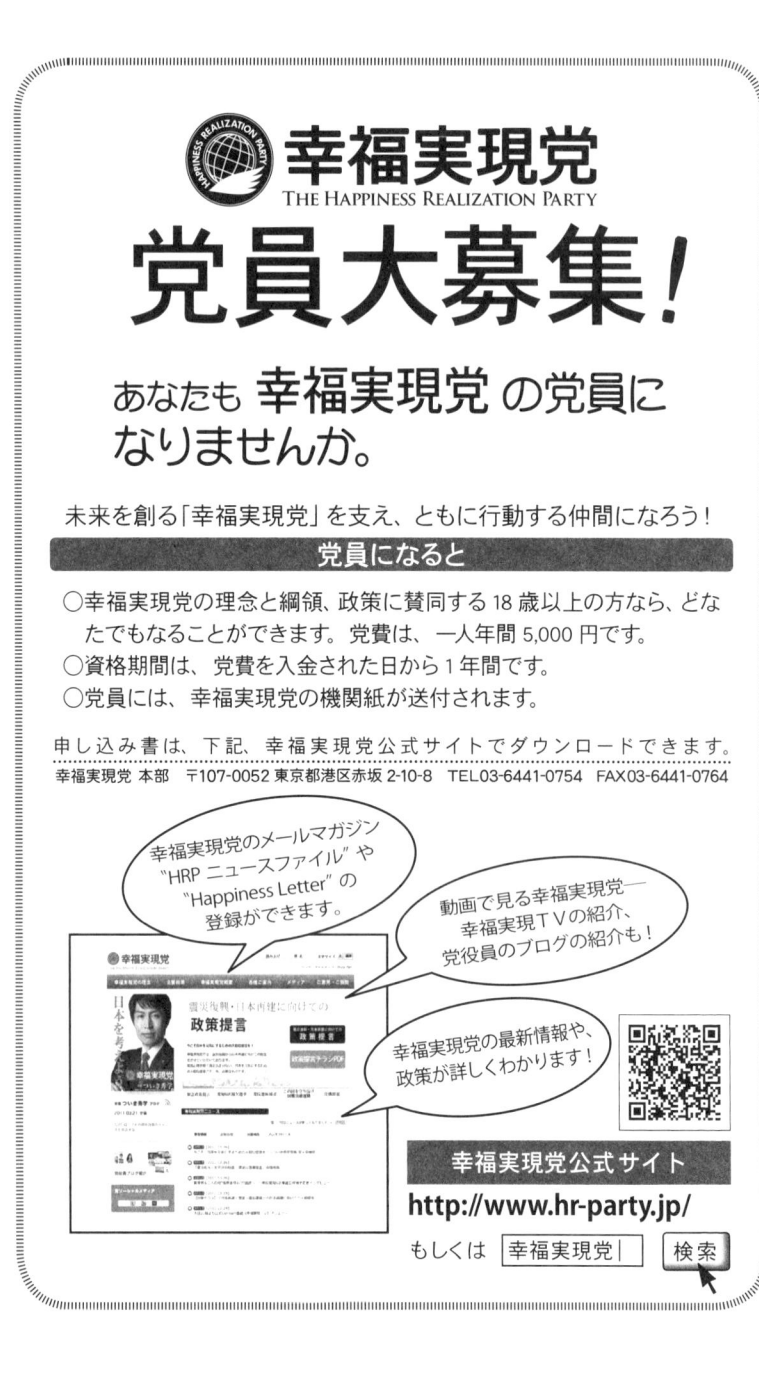

# 幸福実現党
## THE HAPPINESS REALIZATION PARTY

# 党員大募集!

## あなたも 幸福実現党 の党員に なりませんか。

未来を創る「幸福実現党」を支え、ともに行動する仲間になろう!

### 党員になると

○幸福実現党の理念と綱領、政策に賛同する18歳以上の方なら、どなたでもなることができます。党費は、一人年間5,000円です。
○資格期間は、党費を入金された日から1年間です。
○党員には、幸福実現党の機関紙が送付されます。

申し込み書は、下記、幸福実現党公式サイトでダウンロードできます。

幸福実現党 本部　〒107-0052 東京都港区赤坂 2-10-8　TEL03-6441-0754　FAX03-6441-0764

幸福実現党のメールマガジン "HRP ニュースファイル" や "Happiness Letter" の登録ができます。

動画で見る幸福実現党――幸福実現TVの紹介、党役員のブログの紹介も!

幸福実現党の最新情報や、政策が詳しくわかります!

### 幸福実現党公式サイト

**http://www.hr-party.jp/**

もしくは 幸福実現党 検索

## 大川隆法ベストセラーズ・国難を打破する

### 国を守る宗教の力
**この国に正論と正義を**

3年前から国防と経済の危機を警告してきた国師が、迷走する国難日本を一喝！日本を復活させる正論を訴える。
【幸福実現党刊】

1,500円

---

### この国を守り抜け
**中国の民主化と日本の使命**

平和を守りたいなら、正義を貫き、国防を固めよ。混迷する国家の舵取りを正し、国難を打破する対処法は、ここにある。
【幸福実現党刊】

1,600円

---

### 平和への決断
**国防なくして繁栄なし**

軍備拡張を続ける中国。財政赤字に苦しみ、アジアから引いていくアメリカ。世界の潮流が変わる今、日本人が「決断」すべきこととは。
【幸福実現党刊】

1,500円

幸福の科学出版　　※表示価格は本体価格（税別）です。

## 大川隆法 ベストセラーズ・幸福実現党の魅力とは

### ジョーズに勝った尖閣男
**トクマとの政治対談**

尖閣上陸！ なぜ彼は、無謀とも思える行動に出たのか!? 国師との対談で語られる尖閣上陸秘話と、国を愛する情熱と信念について。

1,400円

### 国防アイアンマン対決
**自民党幹事長 石破茂守護霊**
**vs. 幸福実現党出版局長 矢内筆勝**

いま、改めて注目される幸福実現党の国防戦略とは!? 国防第一人者と称される石破氏守護霊の本音が明かされる緊急国防論争。
【幸福実現党刊】

1,400円

### 「人間グーグル」との対話
**日本を指南する**

氾濫する情報の中から、真実だけをクリックする──。国師と幸福実現党政調会長が、日本の問題点と打開策を縦横無尽に語り合う。
【幸福実現党刊】

1,400円

幸福の科学出版

## 大川隆法ベストセラーズ・幸福実現党の魅力とは

### 「アエバる男」となりなさい
#### PRできる日本へ

アメリカ共和党も認めた幸福実現党の正当性！ 国師との対談から見えてくる日本政治の問題点と、国難を打破する人材論とは。　【幸福実現党刊】

1,400 円

---

### スピリチュアル党首討論
#### 安倍自民党総裁 vs. 立木幸福実現党党首

自民党が日本を救う鍵は、幸福実現党の政策にあり！ 安倍自民党新総裁の守護霊と、立木秀学・幸福実現党党首が政策論争を展開。　【幸福実現党刊】

1,400 円

---

### 野獣対談
### ──元祖・幸福維新

外交、国防、経済危機──。幸福実現党の警告が次々と現実化した今、国師が語り、党幹事長が吠える対談編。真の維新、ここにあり！　【幸福実現党刊】

1,400 円

---

### 猛女対談
### 腹をくくって国を守れ

国の未来を背負い、国師と猛女が語りあった対談集。凜々しく、潔く、美しく花開かんとする、女性政治家の卵の覚悟が明かされる。　【幸福実現党刊】

1,300 円

※表示価格は本体価格（税別）です。

## 大川隆法 ベストセラーズ・世界の指導者シリーズ

### ヒラリー・クリントンの政治外交リーディング
**同盟国から見た日本外交の問題点**

竹島、尖閣と続発する日本の領土問題……。国防意識なき同盟国をアメリカはどう見ているのか？ クリントン国務長官の本心に迫る！
【幸福実現党刊】

1,400円

---

### ロシア・プーチン 新大統領と帝国の未来
**守護霊インタヴュー**

中国が覇権主義を拡大させるなか、ロシアはどんな国家戦略をとるのか!? また、親日家プーチン氏の意外な過去世も明らかに。
【幸福実現党刊】

1,300円

---

### イラン大統領 vs. イスラエル首相
**中東の核戦争は回避できるのか**

世界が注視するイランとイスラエルの対立。それぞれのトップの守護霊が、緊迫する中東問題の核心を赤裸々に語る。
【幸福実現党刊】

1,400円

幸福の科学出版　　　　　　　　※表示価格は本体価格(税別)です。